WHO'S AFRAID OF THE
BIG BAD BOSS?

HOW TO SURVIVE 13 TYPES OF
DYSFUNCTIONAL, DISRESPECTFUL,
DISHONEST LITTLE DICTATORS

By

Marilyn Haight

ISBN 978-0-9800390-1-6
Library of Congress Control Number: 2008923581

Cover copyright © 2005 Marilyn Haight

Published by:
Worded Write Publishing
20403 N. Lake Pleasant Rd.
Suite #117-150
Peoria, AZ 85382-9707
Phone: (623) 825-3845
Web: http://www.wordedwrite.com

Worded

Write

Published February 2008

Table of Contents

DO YOU NEED THIS BOOK?

DOES YOUR BOSS:

1. Ignore "people" issues such as support, development and conflict?

2. Criticize, downplay, or ignore your ideas; take credit for your work; or make you to do her or his work secretly?

3. Lack necessary knowledge, skill or experience in your field or profession?

4. Ignore serious problems or make them worse?

5. Measure results based only on things that can be easily counted?

6. Hire unqualified employees, vendors or consultants?

7. Do the nitty-gritty, detailed work in your department?

8. Insult, taunt, harass, or threaten you; or try to intimidate you by snapping, shouting, and/or cursing at you?

9. Expect you to agree with her or his ideas or misguide you?

10. Gossip with your peers or encourage infighting and internal competition between you and your coworkers?

11. Use company assets for inappropriate, unneeded, or poor quality products or services, or disappear for long periods of time during work hours?

12. Work against company goals and programs while pretending to support them?

13. Have different personality traits on different days?

   If you answered "yes" to one or more of these questions,
   this book can help you!

INTRODUCTION

Wallace, the Director of Financial Operations at a large company, didn't like finance. He liked to teach management classes and give advice. Eventually, his position was "downsized." His experience and MBA in Finance didn't qualify him for the profession he wanted to work in, yet he rewrote his resume and marketed himself as an Organization Development specialist.

Sidney, a Vice President at another large company, didn't know what skills the "Director of Organization Development" position required when he interviewed Wallace. He liked Wallace, so he hired him to design and carry out a cultural transition.

Wallace didn't know how to design a cultural transition or how to write the business plan for his new department, so he hired Sally, a legitimate Organization Development specialist. Sally spent many hours teaching Wallace how to design a cultural transition. She wrote the business plan and coached Wallace in how to present it to Sidney. Wallace made Sally delete important functions from the business plan because he didn't understand them and didn't think he could explain them to Sidney. He prohibited Sally from talking to Sidney in his absence.

Intimidated by Sally's knowledge and competence, Wallace built a case for terminating her when he thought he had learned enough. He labeled her as a difficult and uncooperative employee. Sally lasted for four months.

What would you do in Sally's situation?

There are some bosses you can never please. You can try to "manage" your boss by changing your behavior, adopting a different personality style, using fancy communication or negotiation techniques, practicing conflict management skills, walking on egg shells or walking on water, but none of these strategies will work with a boss who doesn't want to get along with you. None of these strategies will work with a boss who wants to dominate you or who wants to get away with something inappropriate. This bad behavior is deliberate; you can't change it, but you don't have to join it or sacrifice your values in order to survive it.

Bad bosses get away with their misbehavior by operating just under the radar screen—they are not so blatant that they are breaking a law or attracting the attention of company officers, but they are not so subtle that their behavior could be called civil or ethical. Bad bosses accept positions they're not qualified for; they hurt the people who report to them in economic, emotional, psychological and sometimes physical ways; and they take assets or privileges they are not entitled to. These bosses are usually pretty smart people—they must be smart to get away with being so bad— so it's not easy to deal with them in a straightforward way.

This book tells you what to do if you report to a bad boss. First, realize that it is not you or your perception that is at fault. Even if you are the only person who experiences your boss in this way, you are not the problem! But once you report to a bad boss, whether the result of accepting a new position or being reassigned, you have only three options:

- Transfer

- Resign

- Stay

- How do you decide which option is best for you?

- How do you determine the best way to execute your decision?

- How can you avoid accepting a job with a bad boss in the first place?

Who's Afraid of the Bad Boss: How to Survive 13 types of Dysfunctional, Disrespectful, Dishonest Little Dictators helps you answer these questions.

The true stories in each chapter can help you evaluate your own situation. (The identities of individuals and organizations have been altered to allow them to remain anonymous.) This book also helps you to:

- Identify these 13 bad-boss types:

  The Wannabe
  The Pretender
  The Dumbfounder
  The Player
  The Manipulator
  The Pilferer
  The Combination-Type
  The Suppressor
  The Confounder
  The Propagator
  The Bully
  The Cult Maker
  The Saboteur

- Examine your relationship with your manager objectively

- Assess your opportunities for acknowledgement, reward, advancement and continued employment in your organization

- Choose an appropriate strategy for dealing with a bad boss

- Prepare to leave when that is your best option

- Maintain your economic and emotional well-being

This book does <u>not</u> explain the reasons *why* bad bosses behave the way they do; insecurity, jealousy and greed may play a part, but that is for psychologists and psychiatrists to explain. Knowing the reasons cannot help you, anyway: you cannot change another person; you can only change yourself—and if you've ever tried to break a habit, you know how challenging that can be. So prepare to do some work on *yourself* to survive a bad boss.

1: THE WANNABE

"Just give me the perks!"

How to Recognize a Wannabe Boss

I once surveyed over 900 managers; one question received the same answers from 99.78% of them:

"If you did not need to work for economic reasons, would you want to keep the job you now have?"

Their answer:

"No."

When I followed up with:

"Would you work at something else?"

100% said they would.

These managers said managing people was "unfulfilling" and "boring." Why, then, were they working in their current position? Because they wanted better pay, benefits, privileges and status. This was their *only* reason for accepting the job. This is the Wannabe Boss—someone who wants the privileges but not the responsibilities of being a manager.

Wannabe Bosses ignore people issues for the simple reason that they don't want to manage people. They don't know how and they don't want to learn; their job doesn't interest them.

Unlike effective managers, Wannabe Bosses <u>do not</u>:

- Show or tell employees how to apply their skills to meet objectives.

- Remove obstacles that inhibit employees' abilities to work effectively and efficiently.

- Tell employees about developments that may affect their work.

1

- Develop employees and create opportunities for them to strengthen existing skills and acquire new ones.

Wannabe Bosses may even boast about not doing these things with statements like:

- "My management style is to throw people into the fire and let them fend for themselves…"
- "I believe in the 'make-it-or-break-it' method…"
- "Sink or swim: that's the best way for people to learn…"
- "Throwing people into the fire helps them build character…"
- "If they want my help, they'll ask for it…"

"Sink or swim" and "trial by fire" and the other so-called "methods" that Wannabe Bosses use are nothing more than blatant refusals to accept their responsibility as managers of people. Managers are paid to minimize human error, not to increase its chance of occurring. But that's just what Wannabe Bosses do! Their negligence harms both the organization and its people; they cause employees to make mistakes, even when those mistakes create needless suffering and increase operational costs. But wasted time and money don't concern Wannabe Bosses—it's not their money!

Wannabe Bosses scorn people skills and call managers who apply those skills "wishy-washy"—their way of saying "weak" or "insignificant." This is just a cover for their lack of interest in studying human behavior and in developing the skills necessary to manage people in humanistic and effective ways.

Effective managers encourage and enable employees, and by doing so they have a greater impact on the organization than most individual contributors. Wannabe Bosses either can't understand this or don't want to understand it. A Wannabe Boss doesn't care about the greater good that *could* be done by employees if he or she supported them appropriately.

Wannabe Bosses become department managers for the compensation, benefits, privileges, and status—not because they are interested in contributing to their organization or in guiding people. The only success they're interested in is their own.

Wannabe Boss Examples

<u>The Non-Managing Managers</u>

In a technology company, specialists with a particular skill reported to a manager with the same skill. The executives decided to restructure one department and create "pools" of people with mixed skills. Individuals would be drawn from these pools on an as-needed basis and assigned to temporary teams to meet specific client needs. Current managers would become "Managers of Technical Specialists" and would be assigned (also on an as-needed basis) to oversee the work of several teams at a time. These managers would report to other managers: "Managers of Technical Managers."

The executives contracted with Morgan, a consultant, to develop competency models (expanded job descriptions) for the positions of "Manager of Technical Specialists" and "Manager of Technical Managers." In the first draft, Morgan included responsibilities from the current job descriptions for supporting and developing people. Comments from the clients were immediate:

"No one would want this job after reading this document!"

One manager called Morgan and explained,

"This is not what my people signed on to do! I gave them the 'Manager' title to reward them, but with the understanding that they would still do technical work and they wouldn't be required to manage people."

After many similar conversations, Morgan realized that "Technical Specialists" were promoted to "Manager" as a reward for excellent technical work in this organization. They weren't expected to assume any managerial duties; they simply kept doing their technical jobs. None of the managers in this organization were ever held accountable for developing, supporting or overseeing the work of the people who reported to them, even though their formal job

3

description included those duties; the reporting relationship was on paper only.

These "managers" continued to do the work they had been doing in their former technical positions. Their only management responsibility to the people who reported to them was to sign forms whenever an employee required authorization. When the technical specialists who reported to these managers needed their support to escalate business concerns or to obtain information or guidance, the managers were always too busy doing their own technical work. Not only was the work of the Technical Specialists not being managed or supported, but no one was managing the Managers either.

So what were the managers' managers doing? They did technical work, too! They attended project meetings and relayed information about project requirements to the Technical Specialists who should have attended those meetings. In other words, these "managers-of-managers" did the work of people two levels below them in the hierarchy. They also bypassed the managers and told the Technical Specialists what to do, but what they told them was almost always incorrect because these managers-of-managers didn't know about newer technologies! Their meddling-instead-of-managing caused needless rework and missed deadlines.

This entire department was made up of Wannabe Bosses—people who wanted the compensation, benefits, privileges and status associated with the job, but not the job itself—the management work and responsibility.

The Indescribable Job

Sometimes Wannabe Bosses become so detached from their responsibilities that they either can't, or won't, describe their job. This became apparent to Nancy when she contracted to facilitate a working session for a group of middle managers who headed several marketing departments within the same international company. The departments had merged and the managers wanted to establish common goals.

After introductions, Nancy asked the managers, "What do you do during a typical work-week?" Wiley immediately shouted out, "We advertise! Haven't you been listening?!"

Nancy responded, "I understand the purpose of your department. What I'm asking you now is how *you* spend *your* time during a typical work day. What are some of the things you actually do while you are working?"

Wiley shouted even more loudly, "Look, do you ever see advertisements for our stuff? That's what we do; we advertise!"

"Who writes the actual advertisements?"

"We do!" he yelled.

"What are the names of the people who write the advertising text?"

"I don't know their names, they report to the managers in my department!"

"So, if I understand you correctly then, it's the specific job of some of the people in your department to write advertising text, but you don't actually write it yourself. Is that correct?"

Wiley snapped his response back,

"Look, we advertise. What else do you need to know?"

"If you don't actually write or implement the advertising yourself, then how is your performance measured when it comes time to assess your accomplishments and determine the amount of your annual salary increase and bonus? How is it determined whether you, personally, did a good or a bad job?"

At this point, the other managers "got it" and tried to explain to Wiley the difference between the tasks his employees performed and his oversight of that work. No one got through to him. He either could not, or would not, describe how he spent his time at work. No one else in that group explained their work either, even though they understood the question. They were either unable or unwilling to describe the specific activities they spent time on in their managerial role.

The Terminators

Some Wannabe Bosses go to extremes to avoid managing people. Samuel encountered a group of them when a Human Resource specialist, Della, asked him to submit a proposal for a basic-supervisory-skills course. Della represented three managers who wanted the course designed according to their specifications. When Samuel asked why they needed the course, Della couldn't answer. Samuel asked her to arrange a meeting with the three managers so he could ask them directly.

Della called Samuel the next day and reported that the three managers had refused his request to meet, saying they wanted only a "yes" or "no" answer to their question: "Will you develop a proposal or not?" Instead of responding, Samuel asked for permission to meet with, or survey, the supervisors who would attend the program. Again, the managers said "No." In his last attempt to understand the clients' needs, Samuel submitted written questions to these three managers, and got the following information in response:

- The department failed to meet operational objectives and the training program must help supervisors solve that problem.

- The program must teach every aspect of supervision.

- The supervisors have an average of twelve years experience.

An alarm sounded in Samuel's head. He doubted whether these supervisors needed a training program at all. First, objectives could have been missed for reasons unrelated to the supervisors. Second, it's unlikely that supervisors with *twelve years* of experience need basic-supervisory-skills training. And last, because of the strange interaction he had with these managers, Samuel suspected a behavioral problem; training does not change behavior—it provides knowledge and skills but gives no assurance they'll be used.

When Samuel raised these points, Della said she could do no more; she needed to know if Samuel would submit a proposal. Suspecting departmental results would not improve as a result of the requested program, and that something inappropriate was going on, Samuel said no.

One year later, Della called Samuel again. Another consultant had provided the supervisory training program just as the three managers had specified. At the end of the classes, the three managers tested the supervisors. Then, they fired those supervisors who got the lowest scores!

After the firings, morale and results reached an all-time low, and one of the three managers was transferred. Della told Samuel that the two remaining managers wanted him to help them develop cooperation, trust and a new plan. Now *they* wanted to meet. Samuel agreed, thinking they might be ready to address their problems more effectively. But when they asked, "What can you do to get these people to move on, stop complaining, and get better results?" he shook his head from side to side and said, "Nothing."

These two managers were looking for another way to avoid doing their job. Wannabe Bosses don't want to change their own behavior; they want to keep getting paid for a job they don't do. Sadly, few Wannabe Bosses ever become effective managers.

What Wannabe Bosses Want from You

Wannabe Bosses expect collusion from the people who report to them. Your job, as Wannabe Bosses see it, is to help them get away with *not* doing *their* job. They want you to leave them alone, especially when you need help or encounter problems. They want you to work independently and take care of anything that needs attention. They want you to find out what you need to know and solve your problems without bothering them, especially "people" problems. If decisions are needed that affect the department, then they want you to explore all available alternatives on your own before coming to them. They want you to identify the best possible solution and present it to them; they only want to finalize the decision.

Wannabe Bosses also want you to do the paperwork that relates to your employment. This means determining your business goals independently and writing your own performance reviews, including all pertinent materials and examples. They want you to present this information to them only for their cursory review and signature so they can take credit for having done the work. These bosses want you to do that part of their job which is dedicated to supporting you as a valued contributor to your organization. They want you to do all of this without letting anyone else in the organization know that you are doing it, especially the manager to whom they report.

Reporting to a Wannabe Boss

Reporting to a Wannabe Boss is like being an orphan and living alone in the streets. It helps to be independent, competent, experienced at managing other people, and good at interdepartmental negotiation. If you also know the policies, procedures, and operations of your organization, and can be your own teacher, guide and evaluator, you can survive a Wannabe Boss with little stress.

People with a somewhat entrepreneurial spirit who are willing to accept boundaries and the status quo, and not propose changes, not even to improve operations, are best equipped to get along with this type of manager. In other words, people who get along best with a Wannabe Boss are those who can perform their boss's job without asking questions their boss either can't or won't answer, and without expecting recognition for it because this boss will not acknowledge your efforts.

If you are new to your organization and find yourself reporting to a Wannabe Boss, you are in trouble—especially if this is your first job. There will be much for you to learn but you cannot learn it from your Wannabe boss. You will be left to flounder about and find co-workers to teach you how to do your job, if any are willing. You will probably make many mistakes before those mistakes are brought to your attention—if you last long enough for anyone to want you to correct them. You will have no way to gauge your performance. Your Wannabe Boss will not tell you that you did a good job substituting for her or him and won't reward you for learning on your own.

Even if you have worked at many jobs before, you are likely to have trouble: every organization and department has its own ways. Managers are responsible and obligated to orient new people to the ways of their organization—but Wannabe Bosses don't want any part of that responsibility. They may assign you to work with another employee to "learn the ropes" or they may just let you flounder. If you need anything from your manager other than superficial friendship or collegiality, then reporting to a Wannabe Boss will be difficult for you.

The Wannabe Boss Survival Quiz

Examine your relationship with your Wannabe Boss objectively in this "True-or-False" quiz:

Statement:	T	F
1. You are very good at your profession.		
2. You keep current in your professional discipline by reading about trends and advancements and by applying those that are relevant to your work.		
3. You belong to professional associations in your discipline and you read and/or contribute to their journals		
4. You need <u>no</u> guidance in how to perform your job.		
5. You have reliable contacts in positions of authority who keep you informed about changes in your company.		
6. There is <u>no</u> conflict within your department that requires a manager's intervention.		
7. You do not need positive reinforcement or feedback about your work.		
8. You do not want a higher-level position now or in the future.		

If you responded "<u>True</u>" to five or more of these statements, you might survive reporting to a Wannabe Boss without experiencing many negative consequences. If you plan to continue to report to your Wannabe Boss, prepare yourself to be able to answer "True" to all of the statements in this quiz.

If you responded "<u>False</u>" to four or more of these statements, then reporting to a Wannabe Boss is probably already very stressful for you. You may find that people in your support network do not believe you when you tell them what you are experiencing. They may tell you that you must change your behavior or attitude to cope. As a result, you may begin to doubt yourself and wonder whether you are exaggerating your situation. You may have difficulty trusting your judgment or remaining objective under these circumstances.

Strategies for Surviving a Wannabe Boss

To succeed with a Wannabe Boss, take steps toward being able to respond "True" to all of the statements in the Wannabe Boss Survival Quiz. For example:

- Work at becoming a highly competent professional in your field through formal study and practice supervised by teachers in advanced educational programs, mentors in your organization, or master-level professionals who will allow you to apprentice with them on the job.

- Obtain degrees and/or certifications where applicable.

- Read books and periodicals in your field regularly to learn about new trends in your field, and apply them in your work.

- Join professional associations that support your discipline. Read and contribute to their journals.

- Take initiative to do whatever is needed in your job and keep your Wannabe Boss informed of your progress through weekly or bi-weekly status reports. Don't wait or ask for direction or guidance.

- Learn the skills of negotiation and arbitration to manage conflict.

- Develop professional relationships with people in positions of authority who will keep you informed about changes in your company.

- Rely on intrinsic rewards for self-satisfaction such as self-acknowledgement for work that is well done or recognition from supportive co-workers and managers in other departments.

- Commit to a career at your current level.

Basically, to be able to work well with a Wannabe Boss you must not need a boss at all. But you must take care to not become so independent that you disregard what your boss asks you to do.

Strategies That Won't Work

You cannot "manage-your-manager" with a Wannabe Boss. A Wannabe Boss does not want to do her or his job, and you have no authority to insist on it. Get used to the idea that this is the way it is. You can only manage yourself.

Escalating your concerns to a higher-level manager is also useless. Your boss gets away with not doing the job because her or his manager allows it. Your Wannabe Boss's manager is most likely not interested in managing people either—otherwise your boss would be held accountable for "people results" and at least go through the motions, pretending to support you so he or she can have a list of accomplishments in that category.

If you've worked in your organization for less than six months and dare to escalate your concerns or complain, then your employment may be terminated without an explanation. The first six months of employment are typically considered a trial period.

After six months of employment with an organization, your employer has accepted you by default as a satisfactory contributor. Your employer has also accepted the responsibility of helping you to continue as a satisfactory contributor for as long as you are able and willing to do so. If you escalate your concerns or complain after this much time has passed, your Wannabe Boss will make your work life so unpleasant in hard-to-prove ways that you'll want to resign. Your boss will not fire you only because he or she does not want to do the work of preparing the required documentation. When you get to this stage with a Wannabe Boss, resigning may be the only way for you to retain your physical and emotional well-being.

Interview Strategies

What to listen for:
- *I'm a hands-off type of boss.*
- *My management style is to let you do your job.*
- *I expect you to take the bull by the horns and run with it.*
- *I need you to be able to hit the ground running.*

These statements may indicate trouble. Let them serve as signals that you need to ask more questions, such as:
- What do you like about being the manager of this department?
- How do you handle issues that are escalated to you for resolution?
- How available are you?
- May I talk with some of the people who already report to you?

An effective manager will answer these questions directly and openly; a Wannabe Boss is more likely to be evasive or to say things that discourage you from pursuing the position.

Accepting the Consequences of Staying

If you responded "False" to any of the questions in the Survival Quiz, then you must recognize that your Wannabe Boss either cannot or will not provide adequate support for you. The support that you need is not otherwise available to you, either. If you cannot or do not want to respond "True" to all of the statements in the Survival Quiz, and you do not want to take steps toward transferring or leaving, then you have chosen your situation. You must accept that *you* subject yourself to the negative consequences you experience. No one can force you to stay in a bad relationship. Unless you reach a point at which you can honestly respond "True" to all of the statements in the Wannabe Boss Survival Quiz, consider transferring to another position within your organization or leaving the organization. Chapter 14, *Basic Bad-Boss Survival Strategies*, provides further guidance for choosing and carrying out either of these options.

If you *must* remain in a reporting relationship with a Wannabe Boss but you cannot honestly respond "True" to all of the Survival Quiz statements, then consider the advice in the Appendix: *Where to Find Help*. There are few reasons why you *must* stay in a bad relationship and many reasons why you may *choose* to do so. Be honest with yourself about your decision and your reasons for making it. If you *must* stay, then consider the situation temporary and work actively toward transferring or leaving, no matter how long you think it may take. Knowing that you are taking steps toward improving your situation can help you remain tolerant for a longer period of time and it can help you minimize negative stress in your work life until you can take the final step of transferring or leaving.

2: THE SUPPRESSOR

"No one here is smarter than me."

How to Recognize a Suppressor Boss

Lea invited the technical staff to a meeting to design a new information-technology application. She asked the technical managers for their ideas. After answering a few questions she began tapping her fingers on the conference table. She interrupted the managers when they spoke and criticized all of their suggestions. Fifteen minutes into the meeting, she stopped tapping her fingers, raised her hands with palms facing the group and shouted,

"Look, I can make this decision in seven minutes by myself! The only reason I'm involving you is because I've been told that people will accept an idea better if they think they were involved in making the decision!"

Lea knew what she wanted before she asked the managers for their ideas. She could have just told them. Instead, she pretended to want their ideas. Lea is a typical Suppressor Boss.

The Suppressor Boss is a one-person-show. Suppressor Bosses assume that no one else in their workplace is as capable or smart as they are. They regard the people who report to them as nuisances—obstacles to expressing their own greatness.

Suppressor Bosses ignore the contributions and ideas of others in favor of their own, and they use others' best ideas as if they were their own. They pretend to be "participatory managers," involving their employees in decision making, but they do so only to get their employees ideas to use as their own. They suppress the talents and abilities of those who report to them by denying them the opportunity to contribute to significant projects and gain acknowledgement for their ideas.

Suppressor Bosses pride themselves on their intelligence, and assume that they are smarter than everyone else in their organization. They use their position of authority to justify that they are smarter than those who hold lower-level positions, and they explain their own lower-level management position as an interim step on their way to the top—where they expect to replace the "dummies" who now hold those higher-level positions.

Suppressor Bosses criticize, downplay, and/or ignore the ideas and suggestions of the people who report to them, even those who have more expertise in the subject. They find it hard to believe that anyone else could possibly offer a better idea than they can. When Suppressor Bosses hear an idea that they like, they take credit for it and act as though it was their original idea. They do this so convincingly that it seems as though they actually believe that the stolen idea is their own. They do not acknowledge others for the significant ideas they take from them, but they do offer feigned recognition for ideas and contributions that are expected or routine. The feigned appreciation for smaller accomplishments is nothing more than an attempt to encourage employees to continue to contribute ideas and, thereby, ensure a continuous source of fresh material for Suppressor Bosses to declare as their own. Employees who receive this feigned recognition are encouraged by the hope that they may one day receive genuine recognition for their significant contributions. This false hope is nurtured by the Suppressor Boss.

Suppressor Bosses continually interrupt people who hold lower-level positions. Their interruptions send the message:

> *"Whatever you have to say is not nearly as important or useful as what I have to say. Shut up and listen to me. I know best, so let's just do it my way and get it done quickly."*

These bosses are frequently heard to say: *"Don't you talk to anyone without going through me!"* Employees are not permitted to talk with their Suppressor Boss's peers or superiors without first asking for their Suppressor Boss's permission to do so. A Suppressor Boss demands to know the detailed content of any communication he or she allows an employee to have with her or his peers and superiors. When permission is granted to talk with these people, the Suppressor Boss will limit what may and may not be discussed. He or she will demand to receive a copy of all written correspondence and to be informed of the details of all spoken communication. This communication restriction minimizes the risk that the Suppressor Boss's peers and superiors might think any of their employees are as knowledgeable and smart as they are. It also minimizes the risk that those people may discover the true source of the Suppressor Boss's ideas. The Suppressor Boss wants to be perceived as irreplaceable.

Suppressor Bosses cannot and/or do not want to foster cooperative interaction among people in the workplace. They do not value different perspectives or accept that differences contribute to better results for their organization. The preservation of their self-perceived greatness is more important to them than obtaining optimal business outcomes for their organization.

Suppressor Bosses do not allow the employees who report to them to exercise leadership; employees are prohibited from contributing useful ideas and managing important projects—the more knowledgeable and competent the employee, the greater the restrictions. Suppressor Bosses perceive competent employees as challengers to their supreme intellect rather than as worthy contributors and valued specialists. Before investigating any issue brought to their attention, Suppressor Bosses will tell anyone who reports a problem to them that one of their employees most likely caused the problem. They accomplish two things by doing this: they appear cooperative to others, and they weaken any confidence others may have in the employees who report to the Suppressor Boss. This strategy positions them as the most likely contact for future interaction and cuts off direct communication with their employees.

Suppressor Bosses may choose, as a "personal assistant," an employee who reveres them and poses no perceivable threat regardless of that employee's legitimate job title. This "personal assistant" usually follows the Suppressor Boss from job to job; the Suppressor Boss always finds a position for this assistant on her or his staff. The personal assistant may be used to spy on other employees and inform the Suppressor Boss of any significant activity that may earn acknowledgement or recognition so the project can be taken over by the boss who wants that recognition for herself or himself. Suppressor Bosses require their employees to educate their personal assistant so that the assistant can educate them with what they learn.

Suppressor Bosses perceive themselves as "leaders" by virtue of their title when they are nothing more than authoritative managers who behave like dictators. Employees do not respect or willingly follow the directives given by a Suppressor Boss in the way they would willingly follow an esteemed leader's guidance; they follow Suppressor Bosses only under coercion (the implied or overt threat of negative consequences) or obligation (the belief that they must do as they are directed by their manager according to the rules of their hierarchy). The mere fact that Suppressor Bosses have achieved their level within the hierarchy validates for them that they are more capable and smarter than others and, therefore, their way is the best way.

Suppressor Boss Examples

The Piggy-Backer

One of the executives at Clarice's organization asked her to work on a high-visibility assignment that involved developing a marketing tool for attracting new executives to the organization. Clarice asked Denise to attend the initial meeting with her to hear the executive explain the assignment. She instructed Denise, *"Just listen; I'll do all the talking."* Clarice introduced Denise as a new employee who was learning about the organization. She said she thought it would be good for Denise to meet some of the executives and hear first-hand hand what they were trying to accomplish for the organization. As they left the meeting, Clarice asked Denise,

"Well, what do you think?"

Denise replied, "That sounds like an interesting project."

"Yes, it is. How would you go about it?"

After Denise made a few suggestions, Clarice said,

"I'm going to work on this project myself. I just wanted you to see the kinds of things that come up around here."

Two weeks later, Clarice assigned the project to Denise to complete. She gave Denise the work she had started and told her to finish it and return it to Clarice. If Denise had any questions, she was to ask Clarice, and Clarice would get answers from the executive.

Denise looked at Clarice's work and asked, "Are you sure this is the work you did for that project?"

"Yes, why?"

"What you've written are instructions for how to do the job. As I recall, the assignment was to develop a marketing package to attract new executives to this position. Did I misunderstand?"

"I was just getting started and brainstorming some ideas when I got busy with other things. Just disregard what I've done. Draft an outline and let me how you would design this package, then we'll talk about it again."

Denise drafted an outline of the marketing package she would propose and explained to Clarice how each section would satisfy the executive's goals. Clarice told Denise to go ahead with her plan, but to give the project back to Clarice one week before the due date. When Denise handed her work over to Clarice, Clarice explained that she was going to make some changes and would submit the completed project herself. She changed a few words, put her name on Denise's work, and submitted it to the executive as her own work. She never acknowledged Denise and never told her what became of the project. This is typical of a Suppressor Boss.

The Protector

Suppressor Bosses can be mysterious and vague when inhibiting employees:

"I understand you sent another letter to the Project Manager."

"Yes, I did. There's still a problem. He's new and he's not familiar with these kinds of offerings. There's an entire aspect of this project he doesn't know anything about and we're not going to be able to deliver the service if he continues to overlook it."

"That's enough. No more letters."

"What do you mean, Norman?"

"I mean that you are not to send letters to the Project Manager anymore. Do you understand me, Shelly?"

"Not really. I'm a member of the team. How can I not communicate with the Project Manager?"

"I didn't say you can't communicate with him. I'm telling you not to do it in writing."

"So what am I supposed to do when I see a problem? The team meets only once a month and we're all in different parts of the country—that's too long to let things go."

"If you see a problem, you tell me about it."

"Are you getting involved in this project now?"

"If I have to."

"I don't see a need for you to have to. Besides, you're not familiar with the offering and you don't know the team members. Isn't it just easier for me to handle things and keep you informed?"

"This is an important project and the Project Manager is well connected. There are things you don't know about—political things."

"What are they?"

"You don't need to know."

"But I'm a core member of the team. If there's information that can help me do my part better, I think I should know about it, don't you?"

"No. I'm stepping in now. Just do your assignments. I want everything to go through me. Don't send any e-mail messages, memos, letters, drafts or anything directly to the team members or the Project Manager. Give everything to me and I'll take care of it."

"Does that mean that you're representing our department on this team now and I'm off the project?"

"No, you've still got work to do. I'll handle the communications."

"But there are things I need to discuss with other team members to be sure we're designing a compatible approach. Are you telling me that I can't communicate directly with them now?"

"Right."

"That's going to impact my credibility with the team. You're putting me in a very awkward position."

"Look, I'm protecting you. I'm keeping you from being perceived as a trouble maker."

"Trouble maker! I'm the most experienced member of the team—I've helped the others get up to speed! This project wouldn't have gotten as far as it has by now if I hadn't helped. How can I possibly be perceived as a trouble maker?"

"Take my word for it: you'll get yourself into trouble if you continue the way you have been. I'll put my name on the communications about this project so that you won't be held responsible for anything that goes wrong. Just do what I tell you and you'll be fine."

The Blamer

Suppressor Bosses punish employees for good work, as Stephan did to Alana in this example:

An executive at an educational organization complained to Alana one day when her boss, Stephan, was away from his office. The seminar Alana had developed for this executive was incorrectly advertised in the marketing brochure. Another department had prepared that brochure and, although it was not her error or her responsibility, Alana offered to investigate and resolve the problem. Because Stephan prohibited Alana from speaking with higher-level managers in his absence, she kept the executive informed of the status of her investigation via e-mail and she sent copies of all her messages to Stephan so he would know what was happening.

In response to her first message, the executive replied,

"This happens all the time—words get changed and no one bothers to get approvals before things are published! This is going to stop now! I don't want this brochure going out to the public!"

Alana arranged for the brochure to be reprinted. Because she was familiar with the content of the seminar, she rewrote the description and sent three samples to the executive to select or modify before she gave one to the marketing department for publication. Within a few hours, Alana had resolved the problem.

When Stephan returned, he read only the executive's e-mail response to Alana's message. He ran into Alana's office hyperventilating and yelled, "I've seen the messages! What a disaster! Don't leave today until I talk to you about this!" and he stormed out.

Stephan went back to his office and immediately sent an e-mail message to the executive saying, "I was out of my office for just a little while when this firestorm started up. The problem is due to Alana's misunderstanding. I'll get it straightened out right away."

Later Stephan read all of the messages Alana had sent him and saw that she had not been the cause of the problem but she resolved it. Stephan waited until the end of the day to talk with Alana. He walked into her office, sat down and waited for a long while before speaking. His only words were, "I appreciate that you sent me copies of all those messages." Then he got up and left. He never apologized for blaming her for being at fault in some way, or for not reading all of her messages before intervening. Nor did he compliment her for handling the situation so well.

What Suppressor Bosses Want From You

Suppressor Bosses expect the people who report to them to help them obtain the adulation and praise of their superiors, or to get out of their way as they strive for that recognition. Suppressor Bosses want your unfaltering admiration, reverence, and subservience. They want you to unselfishly relinquish your good ideas to them and to pretend that your ideas were originally their ideas. They are most happy when you credit them with your ideas before you present them, by falsely but earnestly identifying those ideas as suggestions that the Suppressor Boss had previously presented or inspired in you.

Suppressor Bosses want you to pretend to be less knowledgeable, skillful and clever when you may be more competent than they are. This is very important to them when anyone else is present to witness your interactions, especially higher-level managers. They want you to praise them publicly and openly credit them with significant accomplishments, even if those accomplishments were yours or the work of others.

When you work on anything of particular importance, Suppressor Bosses want you to hand them your work and prepare them to present the details on their own; they want to be in the limelight. They want people outside their department to get the impression that you need their guidance in everything you do. The more competent you are, the more of a threat you are; they behave as though they think you are trying get the attention and acknowledgment that they want for themselves—as though you would take advantage of them in the same way they take advantage of you if you had the chance.

Suppressor Bosses will blame you for causing problems in other departments even when you were not the cause. They want you to take this blame silently and resolve the problem (in much the same way as the Wannabe Boss described in Chapter 1). They do this to appear helpful and objective to their colleagues and managers. They want you to allow them to use you in ways that belittle you and/or damage your reputation so that they can appear to be heroes in any situation.

Reporting to a Suppressor Boss

Reporting to a Suppressor Boss is like being invisible. You must be willing and able to fade into the background to avoid incurring severely negative consequences from your Suppressor Boss. People who are non-assertive and submissive, who are satisfied with the status quo, and who prefer the comfort of routine and familiarity to the discomfort of change and challenge, and who have no aspirations for advancement, reward, or recognition can survive in this type of reporting relationship with the least amount of negative stress.

Trying to impress your Suppressor Boss with your credentials, experience, knowledge or accomplishments will be perceived as a challenge and will incite your boss's anger and resentment. No matter how qualified or competent you are, your Suppressor Boss sees you as "less than" you are. Suppressor Bosses are not interested in what you can contribute to the organization. They hired you only to be one of their stepping stones to the top of the pyramid. If you are highly qualified and credentialed, Suppressor Bosses will pat themselves on the back for having hired someone of your caliber when they talk to their managers, but they do not expect or want you to live up to your potential. You are a trophy that represents their good judgment of job candidates. Suppressor Bosses consider themselves very smart because they are the boss and can reign over someone of your caliber. They behave as though they are more competent than you even when they lack your qualifications, experience or expertise.

You may sense that you are unappreciated and devalued if you report to a Suppressor Boss. You may wonder why you were hired since you do not receive recognition for your knowledge, expertise and significant contributions. You may even feel cheated by a Suppressor Boss who takes credit for your work. And you may begin to wonder how much longer you will remain willing and able to tolerate working under these conditions.

If you are new to your organization and find yourself reporting to a Suppressor Boss, then consider yourself expendable. Your Suppressor Boss will watch you carefully to be sure that you do not overstep the boundaries that he or she sets for you. You will be prohibited from talking with your boss's peers or superiors unless your boss is present. At first, you will be told that these restrictions are due to your lack of experience in the organization and your lack of knowledge about the other individuals. You will be scowled at if you present your ideas in open forums where others are present—that is the Suppressor Bosses' way of getting you to suppress your talent. If you do not take the hint, more restrictive rules will be imposed on you and you may be prohibited from attending meetings or open forums. You will also be denied access to information critical to the successful performance of your job, and required to act only in response to your boss's direct orders—without asking questions.

The Suppressor Boss Survival Quiz

Examine your relationship with your Suppressor Boss objectively in this "True-or-False" quiz:

Statement:	T	F
1. Your boss is more knowledgeable about your job or your profession than you are.		
2. You rarely have good suggestions for improving the operations of your department or organization.		
3. You believe that your boss is supposed to take credit for your work and ideas.		
4. Recognition and acknowledgement for your contributions are not important to you.		
5. You believe that bosses are smarter than the people who report to them.		
6. It does not matter to you that your boss's boss does not know your name.		
7. You are working at your job only temporarily and plan to leave soon.		
8. You are not interested in advancement or bonuses.		

If you responded "<u>True</u>" to most of these statements, there is a good change you might survive reporting to a "Suppressor Boss" without experiencing many negative consequences.

If you responded "<u>False</u>" to five or more of these statements, it is very likely that you will be negatively affected by your current position. Reporting to your Suppressor Boss will frustrate you and negatively affect your ability and/or desire to perform your job well. Frustration results in negative stress and leads to aggression— neither are desirable and both can diminish your self-esteem.

Strategies for Surviving a Suppressor Boss

There are a few things you can do to deal effectively with a Suppressor Boss. However, for these strategies to work you must be willing to accept belittlement, to work below your full potential, and to give your boss exaggerated and undeserved praise.

- Work behind the scenes and do not seek or expect acknowledgement or reward for your contributions, but do keep your Suppressor Boss informed of your progress.

- Accept that your suggestions will be ignored by your Suppressor Boss or reintroduced as your boss's own ideas. Don't be concerned about who gets the credit as long as your idea is used—be satisfied knowing that you made a difference.

- Pretend to be less knowledgeable, skillful and clever than your Suppressor Boss.

- Praise your Suppressor Boss publicly, crediting her or him with significant accomplishments, even if those accomplishments resulted from your work. Convince yourself that it is appropriate for your boss to get the credit for accomplishments in her or his department.

- Alert your boss to opportunities for her or him to obtain recognition from superiors and get special awards or publicity.

- Accept blame for any problems that relate to your work directly or indirectly, even if you are not at fault. Remember that a Suppressor Boss will not admit to being wrong, so pretend you have misunderstood when an error results from following her or his directions.

If you report to a Suppressor Boss and you responded "False" to any of the statements in the Survival Quiz, you will not be able to tolerate your working conditions for very long. To survive this boss with minimal negative consequences, you must get into a situation in which you can work to your full potential and be acknowledged for your efforts. Get into a better situation before you become demoralized, bitter and cynical—it is difficult to overcome the lingering effects of oppression. Consider transferring to another position within your organization or leaving the organization. Chapter 14, *Basic Bad-Boss Survival Strategies*, provides further guidance for choosing and carrying out either of these options.

Strategies that Won't Work

If you complain or express concern about your Suppressor Boss's management style, he or she will cut off your contact with influential people in the organization. This will restrict your access to people who can help you and limit your "escape" routes. Your boss will also take away from you most if not all of your significant projects. He or she will then assign meaningless, insignificant, and/or partial projects to you instead, in an attempt to bore you into resigning. Or your Suppressor Boss may assign you to projects you're not qualified for or have no authority to carry out, or make necessary resources unavailable to you unofficially, all in an attempt to cause you to perform so poorly that he or she can justify terminating your employment.

Once Suppressor Bosses becomes aware of your dissatisfaction, they will caution their superiors to expect you to complain to them. Your boss will prepare her or his superiors to ignore your complaints and to instruct you to go back to your Suppressor Boss and deal with her or him directly. In other words, your boss will make sure that no one will listen to you if you try to complain or change the nature of your reporting relationship, while secretly preparing a contrived case for your termination.

Interview Strategies

What to listen for:

- *I run a pretty tight ship.*
- *I like to stay involved in the projects my people are working on.*
- *Here's an awkward situation I'm dealing with...How would you handle it?*
- *Sometimes we have to do things for upper management that don't make a lot of sense.*

While these phrases don't necessarily indicate that the manager is a Suppressor Boss, they alert you that you need to get more information. Here are a few questions that can help you determine if the manager is a Suppressor Boss:

- What leadership opportunities does this job offer? Follow up with: What are some examples of leadership practiced by your current employees?
- How do you recognize people for doing a good job?
- What do you think would work in the situation I gave my opinion about?
- How confident are you in the direction provided by upper management?

Evasive responses and criticism of upper management strongly indicate that this manager may be a Suppressor Boss; effective managers are open and direct when responding to these kinds of questions.

Accepting the Consequences of Staying

Coping with a Suppressor Boss requires that you suppress your occupational needs and desires for as long as you report to this manager and tolerate her or his false sense of superiority. This is not easy to do and is not healthy over long periods of time. If you do not want to take steps toward transferring or leaving, then acknowledge to yourself that you are choosing your situation. Accept that you are subjecting yourself to any negative consequences you experience in this situation. Negative side effects that spill over into your personal relationships are likely to be the result of your tolerating belittlement at work. You cannot be forced to stay in a bad relationship indefinitely; you can only choose to do so.

If you *must* remain in a reporting relationship with a Suppressor Boss for more than six months, consider the advice in the Appendix, *Where to Find Help*. As explained in Chapter 1, there are very few reasons why you *must* stay in a bad relationship, and many reasons why you may *choose* to do so. Be honest with yourself about the decision you are making and your reasons for it. If you really *must* stay, think of it as a temporary arrangement while you plan to transfer or resign. Knowing that you have a plan to get out of a bad situation can help you tolerate it for a little longer.

3: THE PRETENDER

"I can talk a real good game!"

How to Recognize a Pretender Boss

Luke, a new member of the group, asked his colleague, Bernie, why he had developed a quiz for an online course that tested students on material that had not yet been presented. Bernie said, "I was trying do what the professors do all the time—they ask the students questions and use their wrong answers to teach them the right answers. It's the Socratic Method; I was trying to integrate it into the online courses."

Luke said, "That's not the way the Socratic Method works…"

Bernie shot a look at Willis, their boss. Luke caught the look and stopped talking. Luke looked at Willis, who was staring back at Bernie. No one spoke for almost a minute. Then Willis turned to Luke and said, "That *is* the Socratic Method. We're trying to make the online course seem more like actual classes, so we incorporated it.

Luke replied, "If we were drawing from the students' existing knowledge, I would agree. But this is new material, and forcing them to guess and then get the answers wrong goes against the principles of adult learning."

Willis asked, "What would you do?"

Luke was stunned. Any professional would know that this was wrong! Suddenly it occurred to him that Willis had no background in their field.

Pretender Bosses are technically incompetent. They are pretending to be experts—they want others to believe they are experts when they are not. They use a few "catch phrases," or jargon that is particular to the profession they work in, so they can sound convincing, but they don't know what they're talking about. An in-depth conversation with Pretender Bosses quickly reveals that they do not understand the full meaning or application of the terms and phrases they so casually toss around. They cannot offer supporting details for their decisions or actions. They cannot produce original, effective results, either; they can only copy what others have done, but they cannot determine how relevant the results are to their current situation.

Pretender Bosses do not understand the work they oversee. They lack technical knowledge, skill, experience and/or interest in the discipline in which they work. They want to be known as experts, but they do not want to invest the time and effort required to study, practice, and specialize in a professional discipline. They may be highly educated, but their education is in a different field than the one in which they work. They rely heavily on their educational credentials to convince others of their competence. They may belong to professional organizations in the field in which they work but only so they can use their membership as a substitute for legitimate qualifications. They do not participate in, or contribute to those professional organizations because they have nothing in common with the genuinely professional members and they have nothing to contribute.

Pretender Bosses cannot be pinned down when pressed for particulars. They are very good at convincing the managers they report to that they are knowledgeable and competent in their jobs when they are not. Fast talk, professional jargon and clear articulation are the "smoke and mirrors" these bosses use to trick people into believing them. When pressed for details, Pretender Bosses create a diversion. They may try to convince you to move on to a new topic, falsely assuring you that they will worry about the details that concern you; challenge your reasons for asking questions; mock you for being interested in details; or abruptly change the subject. They find a way to talk themselves out of situations that require expertise they only pretend to have. They contradict themselves, and then vehemently deny that they ever made their earlier, contradictory statements as they try to convince you that you misunderstood them.

Pretender Bosses are very good at diverting attention away from their incompetence. They redirect it toward someone else whom they perceive as a threat to their well-kept secret about their ignorance. They divert unwanted attention by devaluing and mocking the competence of those who have the knowledge and abilities they would like to have—genuine professionals. Pretender Bosses may label highly competent people as "too serious," "too rigid," "anal-retentive" or "inflexible." In this way, they damage the reputation of competent employees who report to them.

Listen for phrases similar to these:

- "We're all learning all of the time…"
- "I'm always open to learning new things…"
- "No one knows everything there is to know about any subject…"
- "I'm not a 'detail' person…"
- "I'm a big picture person…"
- "What would you do?" (in response to a question asked of them).
- "How would *you* do it?"
- "*Why* would you do that?"

These statements and questions are a strong indication that the person speaking may be a Pretender Boss. People do not need to say that they are learning; most professionals enjoy acquiring new knowledge in their field. But Pretender Bosses do not enjoy learning—when they don't know something, they feel threatened. Pretender Bosses have not learned the fundamentals of the profession in which they work and on which advanced knowledge is built. While we may be learning all of the time, we only need to learn the fundamentals once. For example, once you learn the principles of grammar, you know how to construct readable sentences and you can adapt those principles to different styles of writing—you do not need to re-learn grammar just because you are going to write a business procedure or post a message on a website. Similarly, once you learn the principles of adult learning, you know how to teach grown-ups and you can adapt those principles to different subjects, settings, and media—you do not have to relearn fundamental adult learning principles just because you are going to teach a new subject or create a computerized learning program. Methods and applications may change, but principles do not. We are all learning new methods and applications all of the time, but Pretender Bosses are learning the fundamental principles. They admit to this only when they feel backed into a corner and they do so through clenched teeth or stiffened jaws.

When Pretender Bosses say, "I'm not a 'detail' person," they mean, "I don't understand this subject well enough to grasp the details." They use this phrase as a warning or as a mockery of someone who is offering details that the Pretender Boss should already understand.

Effective managers may ask you what you would do in a particular situation as a way of helping you to develop skills, but when Pretender Bosses ask this question it is because they do not know what to do. They need to learn from you while pretending that they already know what it is that you are going to say. Pretender Bosses ask what you would do in a challenging way, as if implying with their tone: "So you think you're such a big deal, do you?" but bosses who are helping you develop skills ask similar questions in a supportive way, as if they are saying: "Why don't you give this a try and I'll help you fill in anything you miss." After you explain what you would do, effective managers compliment you and add their ideas to your recommendations, but Pretender Bosses keep probing for more information and, if they acknowledge you at all, they begrudgingly deliver a feigned compliment. Using their challenging approach, Pretender Bosses not only pretend to be experts, but they also pretend to be supportive managers.

When Pretender Bosses hire competent people, they do so for four reasons:

- To learn from them
- To take credit for their work
- To get them to teach the unqualified employees on their staff
- To impress their own bosses with their ability to hire highly-qualified people

Pretender Bosses do not explain these reasons to the competent people they hire. They expect competent people to work in their department only for as long as it takes the Pretender Boss and her or his staff to learn what they think they need to know from the competent person. At the time they hire competent employees, they have a plan for terminating them or forcing them to resign as soon as those employees have served the Pretender Boss's purpose. Plans for termination include a lack of projects to sustain ongoing employment, and/or planned hostility toward this person, or false charges about the lack of teamwork skills—all to indirectly pressure the competent employee to resign.

Pretender Boss Examples

The Uneducated Adult Educator

Velma is the Staff Director at a specialized business school whose department develops adult education programs for the teaching staff to present to their students. One of the managers of the teaching staff told Velma that the teachers were complaining that the adult students were not "motivated." He asked Velma to put together a package of resources for the teachers to help them motivate their students.

Velma approached Holly, an Instructional Designer she had recently hired, "I've looked everywhere and can't find any books or articles about motivating adult learners. Do you know of anything I can give this manager?"

Holly said, "Before I can suggest any resources, I need to know exactly what's happening: What are the learners doing, or not doing, that makes the teachers think they're not motivated?"

"What do you mean?"

"Well, teachers can't motivate students—they can only influence their behavior. No one can motivate another person. Motivation is intrinsic."

"I don't follow you."

"These adults either want to learn or they don't. No one can make them *want* to learn."

"But that's what the teachers are looking for—it's their job, and we've got to give them something to help them do it."

Holly tried to explain in a different way, "I don't understand the teachers' request because they already have what they need to influence the students' classroom behavior—grades. These students enrolled to get an official credential—they'll do what's necessary to get it if they really want it; they won't want to fail. So I'm not sure what the real problem is."

"But I told this guy I'd find something for him. What can you give me?"

"Let me ask him a few questions first. Then I'll have a better idea about what they need."

"No! I don't want you talking to those people! Just tell *me* what you would ask and *I'll* ask him."

"I've already told you the first question, 'What are the learners doing, or not doing, that makes the teachers think they're not motivated?' The next question depends on the answer to the first one."

"Well, give me a few possibilities."

"But I don't know what the problem is."

"Okay then, write down a few possibilities of what the problem might be and what you would ask in each case. I'll take it from there."

Velma is a typical Pretender Boss. She expects Holly to teach *her* what she should already know. She doesn't want Holly to talk directly with the teaching-staff manager even though Holly is more capable of handling the assignment.

The Erroneous Interview

Some Pretender Bosses are easy to spot during interviews. Meta arrived for her interview as scheduled. She didn't know who her manager would be when she interviewed for the position of Organization Development Director at this large, national company. The Human Resource Manager said,

"The managers who report to the position you're interviewing for are learning Organization Development on the job. We're looking for someone who can teach them. I'm going to introduce you to two of those managers, John and Jennifer. They'll conduct the first part of the interview and then they'll introduce you to the executive manager this position reports to."

John and Jennifer conducted role-play exercises with Meta. They presented several "hypothetical" situations. They allowed Meta to ask a few questions about each case and then they asked her what she would do in each situation. When they completed the exercises, they asked Meta to wait in the conference room while they met privately to evaluate her responses. When they returned, John said,

"We'd like to go over each of the role-plays with you and explain how you did....You handled three of the four exercises incorrectly." After he explained the responses they were looking for, Meta asked,

"Where did you get this information?"

"We've both been in this job for six months now. We created these exercises for the interview based on real things that have happened in some of our departments. Because we actually handled these situations, we knew that the correct answer was what we did in each case."

"Have either of you had any formal education or training in Organization Development or Organization Behavior?"

"No. Our background is in technology, but we've been learning Organization Development as we go along, we're getting on-the-job training.

"Who is training you?"

Jennifer responded, "We've been reading some books and articles, and we talk them over with each other."

"Did the former Director teach you?"

"No. She was from the technology department and she was learning, too. She didn't like the job though, so she went back into technology."

Meta then asked, "How do you know you did the right thing in how you handled these situations?"

John responded, "We never heard from them again."

"Are you sure you helped solve the problems? Did you follow-up with those groups?"

"No."

Realizing that she would be responsible for teaching these managers if she was offered this job, Meta decided to demonstrate how she would do that. So she explained the most likely outcome of the interventions John and Jennifer had made and described what needed to be done to be sure the problems were resolved. John and Jennifer appeared not to be breathing as they listened, stone-faced. When she was finished, Meta asked what other questions they had for her. There were none.

John and Jennifer excused themselves again and asked Meta to wait while they talked privately with each other. They returned ten minutes later, and John said, "We've carefully considered everything you said and we both agree that you failed this part of the interview. We want to point out that you became defensive when we gave you feedback. Your reaction was part of the interview, and that worked against you. We're going to introduce you to Bethany now, the manager you would report to in this position, for the final part of the interview."

After introducing herself, Bethany explained to Meta, "I like to include the managers in hiring their director because this position involves a participatory-management philosophy. I rely heavily on their evaluation in making my own decision. I know the role-play exercises didn't go well for you, but I wanted to meet you anyway to ask what you think of our process."

Meta saw the writing on the wall. Not wanting to waste any more of her time, she was polite, kept the meeting short, and told her recruiter that she was not interested in the position.

The Manager Who Needed a "Right Hand"

When Wallace finally landed a position as Director of Organization Development—his dream job—he realized he had bitten off more than he could chew. He froze when his Vice President pressed him for a business plan and strategies to help the organization change its culture. So Wallace hired Sally to help him out.

Wallace welcomed Sally on her first day, saying, "What I really need is a 'right-hand person,' someone who can fill in for me when I'm not around. I know you're the person for this job and I'm really glad you accepted it."

A few weeks later, Wallace said, Sally, I'd like you to take a shot at drafting the business plan for our department. I have to attend a lot of meetings because of all the changes going on around here and I won't have time to get it started."

"Okay, but I'll need a lot more information than I have."

"Here are the budget figures. You already know what we're trying to accomplish with the cultural transition and you've done this kind of thing before, so just include whatever you think should be included, as if you were in charge, and then we'll discuss it. It's just a first draft. Okay?"

"Will do."

When they met a week later, Wallace said, "I've looked over your plan and I have some questions. Let's go through it together…Tell me why you included some of these strategies."

During their discussion, Wallace asked, "If you were presenting this, how would you explain it to our Vice President who has no background in this kind of work?"

Sally thought she was being tested. She wasn't sure until Wallace could no longer mask his confusion and told her to delete a few critical strategies from the plan. Suddenly she realized that she was not assisting her new boss but teaching him the fundamentals of Organization Development.

Sally prepared the final copy of the business plan and coached Wallace in how to present it as his own work. He was successful: their Vice President accepted the plan.

So, how did Wallace reward Sally? He stopped talking to her and then accused her of being uncooperative. Then he built a case to terminate her!

Four months later, Sally was gone. Wallace went on pretending to know what he was doing by following Sally's plan.

What Pretender Bosses Want From You

Pretender Bosses expect you to defer to them for technical or operational decisions even though they may not be competent to make those decisions. They want you to treat them as experts, even though they lack technical knowledge, skill, experience, and/or interest in your professional discipline. They want to learn from you without letting on that they are doing so, and they want you to teach them subtly, without making it obvious that you are doing so. For example, you might preface what you say to them with: "As you already know..." Pretender Bosses want you to state your recommendations as questions. For example, you might say: "Because the Socratic method of teaching involves questioning students to draw on their existing knowledge, I wonder if you might want to include some questions at the beginning of this training program?" rather than saying: "You need to include some questions at the beginning of this training program." In other words, they want you to pretend you're asking for their help while you are teaching them.

These bosses want you to consult with them about any decisions that you must make in your job, and they want to make the final decision. They want you to provide a cursory, thumbnail overview of the issue, and to "forget about" all of the necessary details. Remember, they are not "detail" people, they refer to themselves as "big picture" people. They do not know how to evaluate complex details, and complete information overwhelms and frustrates them.

Pretender Bosses want their statements to remain unchallenged when they say something that is incorrect. They want you to smile at them and nod with approval when they speak.

When Pretender Bosses accept an assignment that they don't know how to perform, they want you to do the job for them but they want to present it as their own work. They may say they are busy and need your help to meet a deadline. You will be prohibited from asking questions of the person who requested the project and from talking to that person about anything related to the project. You will be required to ask your questions through your Pretender Boss, who will ask them of the project requester and obtain the answers for you. Your Pretender Boss wants you to keep it a secret that you are actually doing the project so that he or she may maintain the false appearance of an expert in the eyes of the project requester, who is usually a higher-level or more influential manager in the organization.

Reporting to a Pretender Boss

Reporting to a Pretender Boss is like being an indentured servant. You must be willing and able to accept that you are being employed as a shadow to your boss and not as a full contributor to the success of your organization. You must be willing to relinquish professional decisions to your boss.

Pretender Bosses mistrust you. They suspect that you lie about your credentials and experience—they expect that you are trying to make yourself appear to be better than you are. They expect everyone to lie just because it's what they do. They mistrust the professional advice you give them because they lack fundamental knowledge to understand how alternative approaches can work. They do not know what it's like to have real expertise, so they cannot comprehend that some people actually do. If you believe you must correct your boss, do so privately, one-on-one, and pretend to be enhancing her or his idea rather than suggesting an alternative approach.

If you have experience in your organization and your abilities are known to other managers, then it is unlikely that a Pretender Boss will voluntarily transfer you into her or his department. If you are transferred to a Pretender Boss, that transfer will usually be the result of reorganization, such as the consolidation or "downsizing" of operations. If this happens, you are likely to be transferred again soon.

Pretender Bosses prefer to hire people from outside the organization who are unknown internally, rather than hire people who already work within the organization. If you are new to your organization and find yourself reporting to a Pretender Boss, then expect your job to be a dead end. Your Pretender Boss will keep you hidden away like a goose that lays golden eggs. You will become expendable as soon as your boss has learned from you whatever it is that he or she needs to know. When you get to that point, a sudden layoff may occur, your position may be eliminated, you may be given no work assignments in the hope that you will resign from boredom, or you may be falsely charged with inappropriate behavior and forced to resign.

Employees who do not want responsibility for the outcome of their actions are best able to get along with a Pretender Boss. Employees who are capable but lack self confidence can also survive in this type of reporting relationship with little negative stress because they are unlikely to feel cheated when their boss takes credit for their work.

If you are new to your job and must rely on your Pretender Boss to teach you, it is likely that you will be taught incompletely and incorrectly. If you are experienced and competent, then it is likely that you will be embroiled in constant battles with your boss whenever you try to do the "right" thing in your job. A Pretender Boss does not understand the potentially negative consequences of not following the principles of your professional discipline, does not know what they are, and does not trust you to give accurate advice. Whether you are new or experienced, your competence will be challenged and diminished in value.

The Pretender Boss Survival Quiz

Examine your relationship with your Pretender Boss objectively in this "True-or-False" quiz:

Statement:	T	F
1. You don't mind teaching your boss while pretending that your boss already knows what you are teaching.		
2. You do not mind having to routinely defend your work.		
3. You do not mind your boss overturning your sound professional decisions.		
4. Doing a good job is <u>not</u> important to you.		
5. Professional collaboration or discussion about work projects is <u>not</u> important to you.		
6. Your professional reputation within your organization is <u>not</u> important to you.		
7. It is okay with you that your boss misrepresents the technical capability of your department.		
8. You do <u>not</u> mind doing work for which your boss will take credit.		

If you responded "<u>True</u>" to most of these statements, then there is a good chance that you might survive reporting to a "Pretender Boss" without experiencing negative consequences. But this is not something to be proud of; it weakens your self-esteem and dignity.

If you responded "<u>False</u>" to four or more of these statements, then it is very likely that you will be negatively impacted in your current position. Reporting to your Pretender Boss is likely to result in conflict between you and your boss, and damage to your professional reputation within your organization. Conflict with your boss is likely to lead to undesirable assignments, undeserved poor performance reviews, withheld recognition and rewards, and being labeled as a "difficult employee."

Strategies for Surviving Your Pretender Boss

If you report to a Pretender Boss and you responded false to at least four of the statements in the Survival Quiz, then transferring to another department or leaving the organization are your best options. Until you can make your move, you must act as if you do not to know that your boss is only pretending to be an expert if you want to get along with her or him. This involves being untrue to yourself, and will result in negative stress over the long term. To get your Pretender Boss to think that you respect her or his competence, use these strategies in the short term:

- Subtly teach your Pretender Boss the technicalities of your work without letting on that you know he or she is technically uninformed.

- Defer to your boss for decisions and let your boss take the lead in your projects.

- Allow your boss to claim your work as her or his own.

- Never interfere when your boss misrepresents the technical capability of your department, regardless of the consequences.

- Accept that your boss will overturn your professional decisions and require you to do things ineffectively because of her or his lack of professional knowledge.

- Function below your full potential to avoid intimidating your boss and having to explain things your boss won't understand.

If you have been transferred within your organization and now report to a Pretender Boss, to survive with a minimum of negative consequences you must disassociate yourself from this person. As soon as you become aware that you are reporting to a Pretender Boss, begin looking for another position before your boss finds out that you know he or she is incompetent. Make your move as quickly as you can—before your boss takes steps toward discrediting you. Pretender Bosses are likely to reassign you quickly if you are unhappy with your assignment from the start. Chapter 14, *Basic Bad-Boss Survival Strategies*, explains how to negotiate a transfer when you are new in your job.

Strategies that Won't Work

Your Pretender Boss's manager is either convinced that your boss is competent or doesn't care. If you challenge the confidence that your boss's manager has in your boss, then you will also be challenging your boss's manager who made the decision to hire your boss. If your boss's manager doesn't care whether your boss is competent, your challenge will be seen as a nuisance and you will be dismissed with no action taken. Your escalation is likely to boomerang and result in your having two higher-level authorities unhappy with you.

It is very difficult to prove the incompetence of a manager who holds a higher-level position than yours because there are few, if any, managers who accept that it is possible for employees to evaluate upwardly within a hierarchy. There are even fewer who would risk their own reputation to support you in trying to reveal your boss's incompetence even if they thought it was possible— including Human Resources Managers who are part of the same management hierarchy and, therefore, likely to defend your boss as if doing so protects the organization.

Interview Strategies

What to listen for:

Ask the interviewing manager questions like these, in a conversational rather than probing way, and listen carefully to the responses:

- How did you get interested in this line of work?
- What kinds of jobs did you work at before you began managing this department?
- Where did you learn your skills in this field (or, if appropriate, where did you get your degree, license, or certificate)?
- What's the biggest technical challenge this position has to deal with?

You must know enough about your field to be able to weigh the manager's answers to determine if he or she is technically competent.

Accepting the Consequences of Staying

If you want to cope with a "Pretender Boss," then you must be in a position to <u>honestly</u> respond "True" to all of the statements in the survival quiz. If you have already responded "False" to any of those statements, then you may find that coping with a Pretender Boss will cause you to be untrue to yourself and in conflict with your personal values. The stress exerted on you by this internal conflict may negatively impact your physical and emotional well-being over time, as well as your personal relationships. It is difficult to feel good about yourself when you routinely compromise your beliefs.

If you must remain in a reporting relationship with a Pretender Boss, then be aware that there is little support available to you other than personal counseling (see the Appendix: *Where to Find Help*). As stated in the previous chapters, there are very few reasons why you *must* stay in a bad relationship, and many reasons why you may *choose* to do so. Be honest with yourself about the decision you are making and your reasons for making it. If you really *must* stay, consider the situation temporary and begin to work actively toward transferring or leaving, no matter how long you think it will take. The knowledge that you are taking steps toward improving your situation can help you to remain tolerant for a longer period of time.

4: THE CONFOUNDER

"Let's do something, even if it's wrong!"

How to Recognize a Confounder Boss

Juan sent a message to Devon, the Vice President of Human Resources at a mid-sized company, saying,

"I have a difficult issue and I need your help. I would appreciate the opportunity to talk with you before you discuss this matter with anyone else in my department. Please call me at your earliest convenience."

Two days later, Devon called Juan and said,

"I don't really know anything about the work in your department, so I can't help you."

"But it's not about the work; it's about hostility and harassment" Juan responded.

"Have you talked about this with your manager?

"My manager is part of the problem."

"You haven't told me what the problem is."

"I'm under verbal attack every step I take—constant harassment…"

"You have a problem working with the people in your department?"

"No, that's not…"

"You shouldn't be contacting me directly, I can't help you anyway. Like I said, I don't know anything about the work you do in your department."

"But according to the Personnel Policy, this is what I'm supposed to do."

"I should know what the Personnel Policy says—I wrote it!"

Confounder Bosses do not like to deal with personnel or operational problems and they are ineffective at solving them. Confounder Bosses jump to conclusions quickly without examining issues thoroughly. They are not interested in critical analysis or problem-solving. They base their judgments and decisions on assumptions, and they suggest inappropriate solutions to problems before those problems are clearly defined.

Confounder Bosses seek immediate gratification. They like to get things done quickly even if those things are done incorrectly. Getting things done is more important to them than doing things right. They are uninterested in the potentially negative consequences of their actions. When they are the cause of a problem, they want that fact to be concealed.

Confounder Bosses procrastinate when problems are brought to their attention. They go through the motions of responding to problems just to show that they have taken some action, but they don't investigate the underlying cause of those problems. They are uninterested or unaware of the damage that can be done when things go wrong or are left unattended. Eventually, they develop "quick fix" solutions that are unnecessary and/or irrelevant while they ignore the more important, underlying issues. Problems in their area of responsibility threaten their infallible self-image.

Confounder Bosses frequently assign the people who report to them to investigate operational problems on their behalf and to recommend solutions. They give the impression that they are genuinely interested in solutions. Confounder Bosses are so convincing that the employees to whom these investigations are assigned believe that their Confounder Boss is sincere about correcting errors. However, after completing the investigations, when employees report the actual cause of problems to their Confounder Boss they are met with disapproval. When Confounder Bosses learn that there really are critical issues that must be addressed, they respond by "killing the messenger." Employees (the messengers) who work diligently to find solutions to problems, as they have been assigned to do, become the target of their Confounder Boss's wrath when they discover that their boss is the cause of the problem. This discovery highlights their boss's incompetence. Confounder Bosses do not expect the people who report to them to actually do as they have been instructed when they are asked to investigate problems.

Confounder Bosses dismiss problems as if they have been resolved once those problems have been assigned to an employee for investigation—they do not want to hear about those problems again. They rely heavily on people who are new to the organization to conduct investigations because Confounder Bosses do not expect new people to know enough about the organization to be able to locate the cause of problems that originate within their own department. Confounder Bosses want to be told that the "problem" was not a problem at all, but was merely a misunderstanding. They want the investigating employee to conclude that the Confounder Boss is wonderful and infallible. Anything short of this is met with hostility.

Confounder Bosses like positive results and spend a great deal of energy on making it look as if they have produced successful outcomes. They deny the failure of any aspect of any project in which they have been involved or in which they have taken a special interest. They do not have the patience to do things correctly the first time or any time. They like to move on quickly to the next new and more interesting project.

Confounder Bosses surround themselves with both competent and incompetent employees. Competent employees are prohibited from doing their job effectively when more time or resources are needed than the Confounder Boss wants to spend. Confounder Bosses keep competent people on their payroll only to use the credentials of those people as support for any action they take. They may say: "I've hired the best people; we know what we are doing" while they instruct or coerce the "best people" to do things inappropriately. Employees who do not know enough to challenge the Confounder Boss's directions are often given blatantly incorrect orders.

Listen for phrases such as:

- "Don't worry about it, I'll take care of it"
- "It's not our problem, don't worry about it."
- "I'm not the right person to help you with that problem."
- "*Now* we've got to do something about this"
- "We've got to look into it this time."
- "Look into this for me."
- "Make it go away."

These phrases indicate that you might be working with a Confounder Boss. When using these phrases to present problems, Confounder Bosses describe those problems dispassionately—as if they are minor annoyances that have been brought to their attention by people who do not really understand the issues. Confounder Bosses provide little information about the details of problems unless they are asked specific questions. They assign short deadlines for resolution, deliberately underestimating the amount of time required to thoroughly investigate.

In contrast, effective managers may assign the investigation of problems to the people who report to them as legitimate developmental assignments. When effective bosses do this, they present all the background information, and they explain some of the ways in which those problems might be caused by operations within their own department. They request that their department be investigated first, and identify specific areas to examine as a starting point. This approach indicates their sincerity in correcting those problems. Confounder Bosses, on the other hand, expect employees to look outside their department for the cause of problems, and they direct employees away from finding fault in their own department.

Confounder Boss Examples

The Questionable Results

Reviewing Sherman's results, his new director asked,

"Are you sure these numbers are right?"

"Yes. Why do you ask?"

"According to these numbers, Associate-level Training Specialists in your department are getting higher ratings from class participants than Senior-level Training Specialists for the same programs. What's going on? Is there a problem with your Senior Trainers?"

"Let me go back and take another look at those numbers. I'll get back to you."

When he saw that the numbers he reported were correct, Sherman decided to speak with the Senior Training Specialists. He called Vera into his office first and said, "Our new director is questioning our results. You need to get your numbers up."

"What do you mean?" Vera responded.

"You need to get better ratings from the people who attend your classes."

"But my average rating is in the 'Excellent' range—well above the 'Satisfied' and 'Very Satisfied' categories. Are you telling me that 'Excellent' is not acceptable?"

"It's not good enough. You have to do better."

"I'm already doing the best job I know how to do. If you want me to get better results, then you'll have to tell me what I can do differently."

"You figure it out."

"I don't know of anything else I can do. I've been getting good ratings for three years; why is this an issue all of a sudden?"

"The new director thinks the Senior Training Specialists are slacking off because the Associate Training Specialists who have less experience are getting higher ratings. You can do better. I have to go to another meeting now."

Vera left the meeting shaking her head from side to side. She approached one of her colleagues,

"Has Sherman talked to you about your ratings?"

"No, why?" Tamira asked.

"He just told me I have to get better ratings because the Associates are reporting higher scores from class participants."

"What brought this on?"

"The new director's asking questions."

"Do you think Sherman knows what's really going on?"

"I don't know. But I do know that he won't deal with it."

"I'm surprised they've gotten away with this for so long. Maybe this new director will shake things up a bit."

"I doubt it. She jumped to the conclusion that the Senior Trainers are slacking off."

"Do you think Sherman wants us to submit false reports, too?"

"I don't know. I don't think anyone wants to know what's really going on around here. Maybe they'll figure it out when we keep losing customers."

"Or maybe they'll just have another downsizing and get rid of the wrong people again."

"Better get your resume ready..."

Sherman's "pass-the-buck" strategy is typical of Confounder Bosses—the current problem goes unresolved, and a new problem is created; in this case, a demoralized staff.

The Training "Solution"

The Vice President of sales at a large consumer-product company announced, "Sales volumes have declined steadily over the past nine-months. I've invited Selena, the Performance Improvement Director, to our meeting today to explain what we're going to do about it."

Selena reported, "Our product trainers have studied this situation and discovered that the Sales Associates are all doing things differently. Some of them are doing very well—selling high volumes and earning high commissions, but most are just barely meeting their objectives or missing them altogether. I've identified a sales training program that can be customized for our products. It introduces a seven-step process for handling sales calls, from initial contact to close-of-sale, and it has a proven record of increasing sales in other organizations that have used it. I recommend we buy this program and roll it out over a three-month period to minimize down time. Do you have any questions?"

Only one manager responded, asking, "Where will the money come from to pay for this program?"

"It'll be covered by the existing training budget."

"Good."

Approval was granted. Ten months after the training was conducted, sales volumes were flat—there was no significant increase. Selena asked the product trainers to observe the sales associates again. When she met with them after the observations, she asked,

"What did you find out?"

"They're not following the seven-step process. They skip some steps and rearrange the order of the call."

"Some don't follow it at all," said another trainer, and the others reported the same finding.

Selena said, "I'm going to hire a Performance Improvement Manager who'll be dedicated to problems like this. His fist assignment will be to find out why the Sales Associates aren't using the seven-step process and tell us what we need to do to get them to follow it."

Two months later, the new Performance Improvement Manager reported to Selena that the reason sales had not increased significantly was not that the Sales Associates didn't know how to make the sale, but that they didn't understand the features of the new products they were trying to sell. They didn't need sales training; they needed better product training.

Selena responded to this news saying, "Just keep that between you and me. What can we do that will make it look like the sales training had a significant impact?"

Confounder Bosses often use training programs as solutions for operational problems, even when those problems have nothing to do with employees' skills and knowledge.

The Disregarded Data

Thornton, The Director of Training, described a problem to Miranda, an internal consultant he asked to investigate the problem,

"We developed online training courses for the sales reps to learn about the products they sell, but enrollments are declining. They're resisting the technology-based training and asking for traditional classes. They like attending classes because it gives them time away from the job and a chance to socialize with their peers."

"What do you want me to do?" Miranda asked.

"Find out what it'll take to get them to use the technology-based training. We've invested a lot of money to be able to produce these courses and we're not going back to paper and instructor-led classes."

"So you want to know what it will take for them to prefer online courses over the instructor-led courses?"

"Yes."

Miranda started her investigation by reviewing the online courses. She noticed that each course included a section at the end for the sales reps to provide written comments. She asked Thornton,

"Where are the written comments the sales reps wrote at the end of each program?"

"I don't know what we do with those. I'm not sure we even keep them. Check with my secretary, Danielle. I remember her asking me what to do with those once. She might know where they are."

Danielle said, "I'm so glad someone's asking about that information! Thornton told me to ignore it, but the sales reps spent a lot of time commenting on those courses and offered a lot of suggestions that sounded really good. I couldn't throw them away—I thought they might be important to somebody someday, so I created a data base and kept them all."

There were approximately 2,000 written comments that outlined significant problems with the online training courses and offered constructive suggestions about how to correct and improve them. Miranda read them all and created a summary. Then she interviewed a representative sample of sales reps from each geographic region. They restated the things that she had read in their comments. They also said that they liked the idea of the online programs because they did not have to take time away from their jobs and, therefore, they could continue to earn commissions (contrary to Thornton's assumption). But the courses didn't include the information they needed to fully understand the products.

Miranda prepared a comprehensive report for Thornton outlining the problems with the courses and she made recommendations for improving the courses. Thornton responded,

"Who else has seen this?"

"The training managers you asked me to send it to."

"Make sure it doesn't go any farther. I can't have anyone else seeing this, and I don't know that your report is correct."

What Confounder Bosses Want from You

Confounder Bosses expect you to ignore problems created within their department. They want you to let them go merrily along their way doing whatever they would like to do without regard for the consequences of their actions, decisions, directions, or inaction. They want you to follow their orders without question, even when they instruct you to do something inappropriately or incorrectly. They want you to withhold your knowledge when you are aware that their actions may cause problems. They want you to acknowledge them for making significant contributions even when they cause problems in other areas of the organization.

Confounder Bosses know that they are doing things inappropriately or incorrectly. Quickly moving on to the next project is one way they avoid thinking about the trouble they may have caused. They want you to pretend that you do not know that they know they've created a problem. Any indication that you do know will trigger their anger, and they will direct that anger at you. They may challenge you by stating that because you cannot "prove" your claim you must be wrong. "Proving" your claim will be difficult because the consequences of the Confounder Boss's behavior may occur long after they did whatever it was that caused or will cause a problem.

When Confounder Bosses assign a project to you, they want you to complete it quickly so that they can take credit for the accomplishment soon. They want you to follow their directions exactly as given without questioning them, even when you know that following those directions may cause problems.

If you are new and just learning about the operations in your department, they might say something like, "Just trust me and watch what happens" rather than explain their reasoning.

If you are already knowledgeable about the operations of your department, Confounder Bosses do not want you to try to impress them with your knowledge or expertise. They do not want you to be thorough, either. They know that you are knowledgeable—that's why they hired you into their department. Now that you are there, just shut up and do as they say if you want to keep your job.

Reporting to a Confounder Boss

Reporting to a Confounder Boss is like being a robot. You must disregard your knowledge and training, set aside your ability to reason, and limit your thinking to the task at hand. You must be willing to follow orders that you do not understand or that you know will cause a problem.

Employees who lack the necessary skills for their work and lack self-confidence can survive in this type of reporting relationship with the least amount of negative stress. People who want to be directed and who are single-task oriented are best able to get along with a Confounder Boss.

If you are not absolutely confident about your technical knowledge, Confounder Bosses will work hard to shatter any confidence you may have, along with your self-esteem. They can cause even the most capable and confident people to doubt themselves at times by irrationally challenging obvious facts and then prohibiting further discussion.

If you are new to your organization and find yourself reporting to a Confounder Boss, expect to be treated with total disregard for your intellect. Your boss will downplay your background and expertise and try to convince you that your knowledge is irrelevant in your current position. Your Confounder Boss will make you dependent on her or him exclusively for direction and will frequently remind you of your subordinate role. This boss will try to convince you that the work you perform in your current position requires a unique approach that only he or she understands.

If you have worked in your organization for a while and have just begun to report to your Confounder Boss, then you are likely to be targeted as a quasi "investigator" as a test of your loyalty to your boss. Confounder Bosses like to test their new employees by assigning them to investigate problems to determine whether they will challenge their boss. If you discover that the problem you are investigating was caused in your boss's department and you bring that discovery to her or his attention, you will arouse your boss's anger and become the target of her or his hostility.

If you have reported to your Confounder Boss for six months or longer, you are likely to become frustrated by working on "fire drills" that consume your energy but waste time and produce no meaningful results or solve no real problems. You will have also seen too much of your boss's bad behavior. For that reason, he or she will prevent you from transferring to departments in your organization that depend on the work completed in the Confounder Boss's department.

Confounder Bosses may require you to make a commitment to work at your job for a specific, prolonged period of time. They expect that by the end of that time they will have broken your spirit and confidence to the degree that you will not challenge them when you move on to other departments in the organization—if anyone else in your organization is willing to hire you once you have become a mere shell of yourself and wasted away your ability.

The Confounder Boss Survival Quiz

Examine your relationship with your Confounder Boss objectively in this "True-or-False" quiz:

Statement:	T	F
1. You are not interested in the ways in which your department affects other departments.		
2. You do not want to know how to solve problems in your department.		
3. You like to work only on new projects and do not see any value in learning to correct problems in old projects.		
4. You do not mind working on projects that make no positive contribution to your organization's results.		
5. You are comfortable doing or overseeing substandard work as long as you get paid.		
6. You are comfortable placing blame on others for the shortcomings and failures of your own work.		
7. You are comfortable giving incomplete answers when asked to explain your department's operations.		
8. You do not feel guilty about overlooking activities that create problems.		

If you responded "<u>True</u>" to most of these statements, there is a good chance that you might survive reporting to a Confounder Boss without experiencing negative consequences, but only in the near future. However, there is a long-term risk for you. Your future with your organization is almost entirely dependent upon your affiliation with your boss. You will "survive" as long as this boss continues to be employed in your organization and you continue to report to her or him. But as your organization grows or changes, you will be ill-equipped to adapt to new procedures and to make meaningful contributions. You limit your opportunities for advancement by narrowing your perspective and scope of interest. You are at risk for being "let go" or "downsized" out of your organization along with your Confounder Boss. You are also at risk for being unemployable because you have few marketable skills.

If you responded "<u>False</u>" to four or more of these statements, you are already negatively affected by your current position. Continuing to report to your Confounder Boss is likely to put you in conflict with your own values and produce unhealthy stress for you. You have limited opportunities to learn and develop new skills or to transfer or advance within your organization.

Strategies for Surviving Your Confounder Boss

Here are a few things you can do to survive a Confounder boss for a short period of time:

- Do not question your Confounder Boss about anything.

- Never bring problems to your Confounder Boss's attention— he or she will only make them worse.

- Avoid discussing details with your Confounder Boss; just provide overviews.

- Secretly learn about other departments in your organization and how your work affects them; do not tell your boss what you discover.

- Make your own decisions about how to complete assignments and report only positive news or what your boss wants to hear.

- Ignore unreasonable demands your boss makes of you—they will fade away without notice.

If you report to a Confounder Boss and you responded "False" to any of the statements in the Survival Quiz, then coping with a Confounder Boss can only be a short term strategy for you. You can survive this type of boss unharmed by getting into a work situation that not only allows but requires you to engage your brain. Plan to transfer before you spend six months in your department (see Chapter 14: *Basic Bad-Boss Survival Strategies*). After six months on your job, it may be more difficult to transfer. People who work in your department are likely to be perceived by people in other departments as incompetent and dishonest—like your boss. Once you acquire that reputation, whether or not it is deserved, your only option may be to leave your organization unless you can find a department that has no knowledge of your department.

Strategies that Won't Work

Explaining to your boss the ways in which he or she causes problems and how those problems weaken the organization will fall on deaf ears. Confounder bosses are either bored by learning how things work or incapable of understanding complex interrelationships.

Don't even think about escalating your concerns. Confounder Bosses preemptively block your opportunity to escalate issues to their managers. They convince you that you are better off dealing directly with them than with their superiors. They describe their managers as intolerant ogres who take severe and negative action against anyone who tries to go around the "chain of command" (sometimes called the "chain of support"). They claim to be protecting you from the wrath of the managers to whom they report, but they are only trying to discourage you from revealing their incompetence. They convince their managers that they are in complete control and caution those managers to be aware of employees who might try to undo their good work. This prevents employees from going over their heads with complaints or concerns—their managers will redirect complainers to the Confounder Boss to address their problem, and you will be right back where you started, only worse off because you will have aroused your boss's anger.

Interview Strategies

What to listen for:

- *I give people the authority they need to handle problems on their own.*
- *People don't usually bring problems to me.*
- *We don't have problems that require my involvement.*
- *I'm busy with my own work and rarely have time to get involved in the work of the people who report to me; I need people who can handle whatever comes up.*

These statements do not absolutely indicate a Confounder Boss. Here are a few questions that can help you determine if this manager is one:

- How is the quality of your department's work evaluated?
- What measures are in place to ensure compatibility of the department's work with other departments?
- How do you handle problems when they are escalated to you for resolution?
- Would you please describe a specific example of when you helped an employee solve a complex operational problem?

Responses that infer that quality is unimportant signal a problem, such as:

- *We don't have to worry about that.*

- *Our work is so different from what the rest of the organization does that there is no need to ensure compatibility.*

Quality is always important, and all work in a department is related to work in other departments within the same organization in some way.

Accepting the Consequences of Staying

There are _no_ good reasons for remaining in a reporting relationship with a Confounder Boss. If you choose to remain in a reporting relationship with this type, you can benefit by at least being honest with yourself. People who remain in a reporting relationship with a Confounder Boss do so because they like the benefits and protection they receive in return for the minimal effort they expend. They become "retired in place" and no longer invest in themselves as employable resources. Some coast their way into retirement. Some rationalize that their Confounder Boss will probably be "found out" and let go. They hang on for years waiting for this to happen while their self-esteem is eroded little-by-little each day and their skills atrophy. Recognize that any negative consequences you experience in this situation are the result of your choices. When the time comes for you to move on, you may find that you are unemployable elsewhere. You may need to obtain new skills so that you can become employable again.

5: THE DUMBFOUNDER

"But the figures say we're doing fine!"

How to Recognize a Dumbfounder Boss

Felicia summarized the concerns the sales staff had about the product reference system in a list of twenty-one problems. She presented the list to the managers who hired her to study the issue.

In high pitched tones and with wrinkled brows and scowling facial expressions, they shouted out at her,

- "Where are the numbers?"

- "Aren't there supposed to be numbers here?"

- "How are we supposed to know what they think the most important issue is—there are no numbers in this report?"

- "Other reports we've gotten from consultants who worked on different projects always had numbers in them. Why don't you have any numbers?"

- "This is pretty useless information without numbers."

- "Just tell us which two or three things to fix!"

They all agreed that they only wanted to know about two or three problems. No one commented about the fact that the sales staff had identified *so many* problems with the system! The managers refused to discuss the individual problems; they insisted that Felicia tell them which "two or three things to fix."

Dumbfounder Bosses measure the wrong things and measure results in the wrong way. They either lack analytic skill—not knowing how to measure performance accurately, or not knowing what to measure—or they do not want accurate performance measurements. The things they choose to measure make their department appear to be performing better than it is. They emphasize quantity over quality. The results they report are simple tallies of easily-counted activities and events. They establish goals for both financial and non-financial events that can be easily "counted" whether or not those "counts" are meaningful. For example, they may report the number of calls taken per hour without measuring whether those calls were handled satisfactorily, or they may report revenue instead of profit, and not consider profit-reducing factors (costs associated with errors and lost opportunities) from their calculations.

Dumbfounder Bosses are good at getting their managers to believe that their department is more successful than it actually is. They present their results in convincing but misleading ways that can dumbfound their audience. They omit information that suggests they are not as successful as their numbers indicate.

Dumbfounder Bosses either do not know how or do not want to know how to construct narrative questionnaires or surveys, because the results of those non-numerically-based instruments are difficult to tally. Narrative comments that must be read and analyzed are either not requested in their surveys or are discarded in favor of checklists that can be simply counted. They design (or approve) feedback surveys that limit the number of responses and provide simple numerical scoring that can be easily skewed in their favor.

Dumbfounder bosses hold employees accountable for trivial activities. They disregard significant performance issues that affect the quality of work and the impact that work may have on customers or service recipients. When contradictions or questions arise about the accuracy or validity of the results for work performed in their department, they skirt the issue.

They avoid discussions about quality and encourage discussions about quantity. Dumbfounder Bosses challenge the people who report to them to find ways to "make the numbers look good" rather than to find ways to improve quality or do a better job. They say things like:

- "Just look at my numbers if you want to see how well I'm doing."

- "Figures don't lie."

- "Here it is in black and white."

- "If we had a problem, I'd be the first to know."

- "Find a way to get these numbers up."

- "Don't let me hear about any problems with our results."

- "Find a way around it."

When using these phrases, Dumbfounder Bosses speak forcefully, as if they are trying to shut down the conversation. They try to discredit and/or intimidate anyone who questions their results, including the managers to whom they report. Dumbfounder Bosses convince their managers that the managers do not know business operations well enough to understand the reported results—sadly, this is often true. Dumbfounder Bosses tell the people who report to them that it is the boss's job to be concerned about results and not theirs, thereby shutting-down conversation about meaningful measurements.

Dumbfounder Boss Examples

<u>You Get What You Ask For</u>

Thornton, the Director of Product-Training Development, told the Training Developers and their managers that he didn't care what they did as long as they met this one goal:

"Make our customers happy."

But he wasn't talking about *real* customers— he was talking about the Product Managers in other departments.

"I don't want to hear any complaints from those people. That's how I'll know you're doing your jobs."

The Training Developers started writing whatever the Product Managers wanted them to say. The Product Managers instructed the Training Developers to write technical specifications rather than information explaining how customers could actually use those products.

Eighteen months later, sales for new products fell far below projected levels; revenue was declining steadily. The Product Managers pressured the Sales Staff to work harder, but the Sales Staff didn't know how to explain the new products to potential customers—the training they received did not include those details!

While business was fading away, Thornton and his staff flourished. At a staff meeting, he said,

"The outlook for the business overall isn't very good, but our department has done an outstanding job of meeting its objectives! The Product Managers are very happy with the training you've produced, and your bonuses reflect this success!"

Thornton got just what he asked for—happy colleagues. Unfortunately, the happiness of managers in other departments was an irrelevant measurement. That which was measured was accomplished, but at a great cost to the organization; its capacity to sell new products was diminished.

The Intangible Stuff

A group of Engineering Directors planned to establish goals for the Engineering Managers who report to them. They hired Gwen to facilitate their annual goal-setting meeting. After introductions, Gwen got the working session started by asking:

"What are the responsibilities of the Engineering Managers—the people who oversee the work of the Engineers in your business unit—and how do you measure their effectiveness and efficiency?"

The Directors called out several types of jobs that engineers perform while Gwen listed their responses on easel paper. Their responses included activities such as getting jobs completed on time, within budget, and without error.

Gwen posted their list at the front of the room and said,

"These look like the responsibilities of the engineers, not their *managers*. Is this really what the Engineering Managers do?"

Timothy, one of the Directors, responded,

"The managers are responsible for making sure that the Engineers do these things. We take an average of those results to determine how well each manager's group is performing."

"So you average the countable results of the engineers' work to assess the managers' performance?"

"Right."

"Hmm. What does the cumulative count of the work performed by the engineers tell you about how effectively the Engineering Managers supported and enabled those people?"

A long silence followed. Then Timothy said,

"These are the only things we can actually count. A manager's job involves a lot of intangible things—'soft' skills.' We can't measure that stuff."

"Are you saying that you cannot *count* a manager's performance?"

"Yes, that's exactly what our problem is. We can count things we can see and touch, but we can't count this 'soft skills' stuff."

The others nodded in agreement.

"Do you consider only the *quantity* of performance to be important and not the *quality*?" Gwen asked.

"No. Our work is a hard science—we have instruments for measuring the quality of jobs delivered to customers. Managers either do the job or they don't."

"Okay, let me you ask a different question: Are there good managers and bad managers?"

"Sure."

"How do you know?"

"We hear their employees complaining about them."

"What do they complain about?"

"Oh, their bosses don't help them solve problems; don't coach them on new jobs; don't evaluate them fairly; aren't available when they need them—that sort of thing."

"Are those the kinds of things that distinguish good managers from bad managers?"

"Yeah."

"Do you award pay raises and bonuses based on the complaints of employees?"

"Of course not; that's why we count results—we figure the people who report to the good managers are doing a better job."

"Have you ever reported to a bad manager, yet did a good job?"

"Yep."

"Then how accurate would you say your measurement is for managerial performance?"

"Hmm. Not too, I guess. So what do we do?"

"Let me ask you another question before I answer that: Are the activities the employees complain about included in the Engineering Managers' job description?"

"Yes."

"Then that's what you must measure. Managers have one foot in the *quantitative*, technical world—the physical sciences— and one foot in the *qualitative*, people- management world—the behavioral sciences. You are experts at *quantitative* measurements, but you must establish *qualitative* measurements for the intangible, people-oriented tasks; measurements that answer questions like:

'How well?;' 'What kind?;' 'What attributes?;' and 'Of what significance?'"

"That's hard to do."

"It's more involved than counting, but you already know what constitutes good and bad management. Now you must ask yourselves: 'How well are we managing the managers, and what do we expect them to do?'"

"But you don't understand...we're *engineers*!"

What Gets Measured Gets Done

One caller's inquiry to a health insurance company went like this:

"Hello, I just received a statement and I see that your company paid the lab for four of eight procedures, but it doesn't say which ones. Can you tell me which four procedures were not paid for so I can submit a claim to my secondary carrier?

A Customer Service Representative (CSR) responded,

"We don't have that information."

"Don't you have a copy of the statement?"

"No, we only have a copy of the total bill."

"Does it list the eight separate procedures and the charges for each of them?"

"No."

"Then how did your company know which procedures to pay for and which ones to deny?"

"They just pay what's eligible."

"How did they know which procedures were eligible and which were not?"

"The people who make the payments know that."

"Would you please transfer me to someone in that department?"

"I can't do that. They don't take calls. We handle the calls here."

"But you don't have the information I need. How else can I get it?"

"You need to call the service provider."

"I've already talked with service provider. They told me to call you. They don't know which of the procedures they received payment for."

"The provider should be able to tell you that."

"Wait a minute, let me see if I understand this: Your company got a bill from a service provider and paid for some of the procedures on that bill but not others, and you can't tell me which ones were paid for and which ones were not?"

"Not from the information I have here."

"Okay, then, I'll hold on while you check with someone in the department that has the information."

"You can't hold on. This line has to be freed up for other calls."

"How can you take other calls while you're talking to me?"

"I've already told you that you need to call the service provider."

"But *I've* already told *you* that I *did* talk to the service provider and they told me to call *you*. I need to know which procedures your company didn't pay for. They don't know that."

"I told you, we don't have that information here."

"Then, can you get it from wherever it is and call me back?"

"I can't call you back. I don't have an outside line."

"May I please talk to your supervisor?"

The CSR transferred the caller to another CSR—not to a supervisor. The conversation that followed was a repeat of the first one. Frustrated, the caller hung up without getting an answer.

These Customer Service Representatives report to Dumbfounder Bosses. How can you tell? They produce the results that their bosses measure and reward: quickly-completed calls handled without escalations to supervisors. The conversation would have gone differently had these CSRs been rewarded for answering customers' questions—a more difficult but meaningful performance measurement.

What Dumbfounder Bosses Want From You

Dumbfounder Bosses want you to help them appear to be the kind of manager who can get results. They expect you to ignore their inability or lack of interest in analyzing job performance and establishing meaningful measurements for the department. They want you to provide numerical results that make the department look good and that are easy to obtain and explain. They want you to ignore quality issues that are difficult to measure even when quality is the most meaningful way to measure the results of your department's operations. They want you report only that which is positive or can be made to look positive. For example, handling many calls in a short period of time can look like a positive result as long as the quality of the interaction with customers is not considered.

Dumbfounder Bosses want you to lie, or at least not tell the whole truth, when actual results are not as good as they want them to be, but they will not say so directly. They want you to get the gist of their message without openly acknowledging that you may have to falsify or skew information to report the results they want. They want you to report that you have met or exceeded goals in quantities that are higher than past performance results, and to use whatever devices you can conjure up to indicate that some level of improvement has been achieved. They want you conceal important information that indicates performance is not meeting the expectations of those who use your department's products or services. They want you to omit facts from your results reports that may make them look bad.

When Dumbfounder Bosses ask you for results, they want you to present those results to them in easy-to-scan lists that answer questions such as:

- "How many?"
- "How much?"
- "How well?"
- "To what level?"
- "How quickly?"
- "By when?"

They want you to emphasize efficiency, which is typically measured by quantity, and disregard effectiveness, which is typically measured by quality. They do <u>not</u> want you to provide information that must be read rather than scanned, in other words, they don't want you to provide information that answers these questions:

- "What kind?"
- "What features?"
- "What attributes?"
- "Of what significance?"
- "How well?"

These questions describe effectiveness, which is more difficult to understand, analyze, and falsify. Dumbfounder Bosses want you to pay attention only to short-term, internal results. They want you to disregard long-term results and the impact of ineffective work. Whether you work in a for-profit or non-profit organization, Dumbfounder Bosses want the same thing from you.

Reporting to a Dumbfounder Boss

Reporting to a Dumbfounder Boss is like pretending that you do not see that an accident is about to happen. You must pretend to be ignorant, adopt a near-sighted view of your department's contributions, and set aside your analytical ability and knowledge of processes. You must try to convince yourself that you do not know what is happening, and you must cooperate with a boss whose methods may be non-professional and/or less than honorable.

If you are new to your organization and find yourself reporting to a Dumbfounder Boss, expect to be required to work as if you are wearing blinders. You will be prohibited from examining or fully understanding the way in which your department contributes to the organization. You will be discouraged from considering the "big picture" and that may limit your opportunities for transfer and advancement in your organization.

If you have reported to your Dumbfounder Boss for six months or longer, then you may have developed bad habits without realizing it. You may have internalized the belief that superficial measurements are an effective way to measure performance results. It may be difficult for you to unlearn the habit of reporting qua*n*titative measurements of efficiency and ignoring qua*l*itative measurements of effectiveness.

If you have not accepted your boss's methods of measuring performance after six months, then you're fighting a losing battle. Everything you do to emphasize quality will be misconstrued as a negative activity or as a personal attack on your Dumbfounder Boss. The better the quality of your work, the more likely it is that you will be punished for your performance. High-quality work requires time and effort, both of which tend to lower the average of your boss's preferred measurements. Your boss is likely to rate your work as less than satisfactory if it lowers the average. This will limit your opportunities for transfer or promotion, even though you may deserve recognition and rewards. To counter this effect, you may request commendations from the recipients of your work, but your boss will belittle you for doing so and accuse you of wasting both your time and the time of those who provide the commendations.

You may feel unfulfilled in your work and unappreciated if you report to a Dumbfounder Boss. You may be staying in your job because you like the work and are hoping that you will get the opportunity to do a high-quality job. If achieving your standards conflicts with obtaining the results your Dumbfounder Boss wants you to report, then it is unlikely that you will get that opportunity.

The Dumbfounder Boss Survival Quiz

Examine your relationship with your Dumbfounder Boss objectively in this "True-or-False" quiz:

Statement:	T	F
1. You are not interested in the long-term success of your organization or the opportunity for ongoing employment there.		
2. You plan to resign within six months.		
3. You do not believe that performance measurements can help your organization to be successful.		
4. You are willing to misrepresent facts on behalf of your boss.		
5. You are willing to conceal important information to cover for your boss.		
6. You are willing to omit important information about the results of your work to make yourself look good.		
7. You do not care whether customers or other recipients of the work you produce are dissatisfied with that work.		
8. You are willing to overlook serious and/or harmful mistakes and deficiencies in the work that is produced in your department.		

If you responded "<u>True</u>" to most of these statements, then there is a good chance you might survive reporting to a "Dumbfounder Boss" without experiencing much negative stress, <u>but only in the short term</u>. Your continued employment in your current position is directly linked to your affiliation with your boss. You can cope with this type of boss without experiencing negative consequences only as long as you and your boss continue to work together and you continue to cooperate with her or his methods. Your current boss may even promote you, but you will be ill prepared to manage effectively in your next assignment. You will not have learned a discipline for ensuring the long-term success of a department or organization, and you may cause your department to be eliminated or outsourced.

If you responded "<u>False</u>" to one or more of these statements, then it is very likely that you are already negatively impacted in your current position. You are likely to be tormented by a conflict with your values and to experience unhealthy stress and stress-related illness as a result.

Strategies for Surviving Your Dumbfounder Boss

If you report to a Dumbfounder Boss and you responded "False" to any of the statements in the Survival Quiz, then transferring or leaving your organization are your best options. Surviving this type of boss involves getting yourself into a work situation that is compatible with your values. Plan to transfer to another department as soon as your boss lets you know that you must compromise your work standards, and before your boss is fully aware of your disapproval of her or his methods. State that your reason for requesting a transfer is your interest in developing different skills and learning different parts of your organization's operations. Do not mention your disapproval of your boss's methods—your boss may prohibit your move or give a false, negative report about your character if he or she is aware of your criticism. Your boss may be envious of your knowledge, skills and/or values, so any professional reason for wanting to leave the department may threaten her or him unless it is positioned as a developmental opportunity for you.

To get by in the short term while finding another job or waiting for your boss to leave, here are a few things to do to get along with your Dumbfounder Boss:

- Accept the performance measurements your boss establishes; don't question or challenge them.

- Create your own goals that integrate quality with quantity; work to achieve those goals but do not share that information with your boss.

- Establish informal agreements with people in other departments. Get feedback directly from them so you can make qualitative adjustments in your work without your boss knowing.

- Develop an informal network with your colleagues for ensuring that you're your department's results will be effective as well as efficient, and keep your boss out of those discussions.

- Don't be surprised when your boss to tries to involve you in situations that conflict with your values; find a way to satisfy your boss's demands without compromising your integrity, even if that means working longer hours without compensation—remember, it's just a temporary situation.

Chapter 14, *Basic Bad-Boss Survival Strategies*, explains how to go about transferring to another department. If transferring is not an option, then update your resume and begin an external job search.

Strategies that Won't Work

Escalations are likely to be met with disbelief because upper management sees only positive results coming from your boss's department. Upper management is aware of the quantitative measures being reported and, as long as customer complaints are not getting through to them, they see no reason to pursue quality issues. They may say: "Until our customers are dissatisfied, there's no reason to do anything differently." Your word alone is not enough to convince them that customers are dissatisfied, and much time may pass before the negative consequences of your boss's actions and directions become apparent. Unfortunately, it may be too late by then for upper management to respond effectively.

Trying to convince your boss to establish different measurements will also fail. Your Dumbfounder Boss is trying to establish a reputation for getting results that upper management favors. He or she is not receptive to any plan that requires more time or effort. This boss is only interested in personal image—not the organization, its customers, or its employees.

Interview Strategies

What to listen for:

Ask the following questions and listen carefully to the manager's answers:

- What kinds of measurements do you use to report results for your department and for individuals?
- How do you determine whether a job was done well?
- What do you expect employees to do when they recognize that a potential problem may result from their work?

An effective manager will be more than willing to discuss how results are measured and will want to know that you are interested in meeting high standards. A Dumbfounder Boss will skim over the subject or make measurements seem unimportant.

Accepting the Consequences of Staying

If you *must* remain in a reporting relationship with a Dumbfounder Boss, or if you choose to do so, then try to find a way to be true to your values in your work and, at the same time, to honestly report only those results your boss wants to see. To do this, you may need to devote more of your personal time to your work without any acknowledgement or extrinsic reward. This will provide you with the intrinsic reward of satisfaction with a job well done.

There is little external support available to you other than counseling or talking with family and friends because you are not being directly harmed by your boss's actions (see the Appendix: *Where to Find Help*).

6: THE PROPAGATOR

"Be like me."

How to Recognize a Propagator Boss

"Sara, I'm looking for an assistant and I like your style. What do you say—do you want to work for me?"

"That's very flattering, Ned, but I'm so new here and there's so much to learn! It seems like I can learn a lot in the job I have now, especially about the different departments."

"Look, come and work for me and I'll teach you everything you need to know. You'll learn a lot faster from a mentor than you will in an entry level job like the one you've got."

"Are you sure? There are so many good people around here—so much more qualified that me. I don't even have a college education. Why me?"

"They're not as qualified as you think. They know the old ways, but things are changing around here. I want someone I can teach my way and someone I can trust to keep their eyes and ears open to what's going on. You've picked up quite a lot in the short time you've been here. You have a knack for getting the information you want and using it to your advantage…"

"But, I'm only trying to do a good job."

"That may be, but you're ambitious, too, I can see it. How much longer do you think you're going to be happy in your job?"

"Well, I *was* getting bored, but I've taken on some additional responsibilities…"

"See, that's what I mean. That's just what I'm looking for."

Ned got promoted twice during the next two years. Sara got promoted, too, and transferred with Ned as his personal assistant on each of his new jobs. Three years after she started working in the company, Sara held a position two levels above the manager who hired her into the company.

Propagators Bosses hire people who are like them. Whether they're hiring employees, contractors or consultants, they look for the same type. Propagator Bosses hire people they think will help them achieve their personal goals. They hire their personal friends, people to whom they owe favors, people from whom they want favors, people who are associated with others from whom they want favors and people they can make indebted and loyal to them. They hire vendors who are friendly toward them even when those vendors are incapable of meeting the organization's needs. They hire consultants who will help them conceal their ineffectiveness and support their inappropriate behavior.

Propagator Bosses have limited knowledge and experience in the profession they work in. They may have acquired their limited knowledge through informal methods, such as observation of others, limited reading, and participation in substandard programs; or through a formal program they did not complete or in which they barely met the minimum requirements, such as academic-degree programs and professional-certification programs.

Propagator Bosses may also have received a formal education in an unrelated or marginally related subject area and done very well. They rationalize that their academic accomplishment indicates they are smart enough not to need specialized training. They speak to others condescendingly, assuming that the people they meet are of inferior intellect. To conceal their weak or lacking background, Propagator Bosses withhold information about their experience and training when the topic comes up in conversation, and redirect the conversation by describing something else about themselves that is impressive but unrelated. They may say formal qualifications are not important; they expect you accept without question that they are qualified.

These bosses want to direct everything that is done in their department. They don't want suggestions from the people who report to them. They keep employees "in the dark" about what is going on in the organization. They do not want their employees to have information they can use to make helpful suggestions.

Propagator Bosses are very good at marketing their image. They are very political in a self-serving way and trade "favors"—favors that make them look good at the expense of the organization and its stakeholders, including customers, investors and contributors. They tend to be quiet and reserved in the presence of higher-level managers until it is their turn to speak. When presenting, they put on an impressive show and cover all points related to their topic, leaving no room for challenges. They dress in finely-tailored business attire and, on dress-down days, they stand out from the crowd in finer casual clothing or slightly dressed-down business attire (suit pants or skirt with no jacket; open collar dress shirt or blouse; fine loafers rather than more casual shoes).

Propagator Bosses are especially adept at misleading people they perceive as competitors in their race to the next level in the hierarchy. They block access to needed resources by developing relationships with resource providers and then turn those resource-providers against work associates they compete against. They offer to "help" others who are working on projects that have the attention of higher-level managers in an attempt to take those projects as their own, or they may partner to share in the recognition if they can't "own" the project.

Propagator Bosses position themselves as "mentors" to the employees they hire. They offer to guide those employees and "take care of them." Propagator Bosses offer this "protection" for as long as their "mentees" are unquestioningly loyal to them. When Propagator Bosses move on to a new position or organization, they take their mentees with them. They create a new position for their mentees when one is not already available. When they get promoted, they may first back-fill the position they vacate by promoting a mentee into it, and then, soon thereafter, transfer the mentee into their new department.

Listen for phrases similar to these:

- "That's the way we do things here…"
- "We do things my way around here…"
- "That's the company way…"
- "People who already have experience bring bad habits with them…"
- "I like people to learn my way of doing things…"
- `"Just stick with me…"
- "Follow my lead and you'll be fine…"
- "You don't fit the company mold…"

These statements are a strong indication that the person speaking is a Propagator Boss. The "that's the way…" statements are the Propagator Boss's way of telling anyone who is questioning them to back off. These statements are made quickly and abruptly, or slowly and emphatically, accompanied by long stares and direct eye-contact. During interviews with potential employees, Propagator Bosses use these expressions to test the willingness of candidates to unquestioningly cooperate with them, and to discourage highly-qualified, ambitious candidates from pursuing the position. This is how they build their own self-serving "little empire" within the organization but they do so at the cost of depriving their organization of the best possible candidates.

Propagator Boss Examples

<u>Wanted: Unqualified Candidates Only</u>

"…Hello, Ally. It's nice to meet you. Tell me why you're interested in applying for this position."

"Hello, Sherman; it's nice to meet you, too. I'm not sure that I'm ready to apply. The job seems to be in my field, but the ad didn't provide much detail so I thought I'd meet with you to learn more about it."

"It's a typical internal Organization Development job."

"Would you mind explaining what you mean by "typical"? I'm asking because the term "Organization Development" is sometimes used to mean different things: in some cases it means advising and facilitating change initiatives, but some managers use it as a label for project management—for implementing predetermined programs. That's why I wanted to meet with you first—to find out what kind of work is involved."

"Fair enough. The position reports to me but it supports the Vice President of one of our business units—we think of him as our "client." He's recently restructured his department and his managers are making operational changes as they go along. He needs someone to work with the managers who are implementing those changes."

"If they've already restructured, then they must have worked with someone during that process. Is that person still involved?"

"They worked with one of my OD people. She's no longer with the company; that's why this position is available."

"She left in the middle of the project?"

"Unfortunately, yes."

"It's unusual for an OD consultant to leave in the middle of a project. What was her role in the restructure?"

"To tell you the truth, she didn't see eye-to-eye with the VP and he was not satisfied with her performance. I'm looking for someone who can do the job *and* get along with the VP. Tell me something about your experience."

"I've been an OD consultant for ten years. I've worked as both and external consultant and internal consultant. I've helped groups with departmental restructures, starting with the initial concept and supporting them through implementation."

"Who did you take your direction from?"

"No one. I was the primary consultant. I advised the groups, facilitated their interaction, and provided on-the-spot training when they got stuck and needed to learn different skills to continue their work."

"That's too bad."

"What do you mean?"

"I've found that people who have your kind of experience tend to bring a lot of bad habits with them. I prefer to hire people who are blank slates and teach them my way."

"I'm flexible enough to use different strategies. What is your way?"

"Our job is to keep the Vice President happy. Period. He tells me what he wants you to do and when he wants you to do it. I tell you and you do the work."

"Is he an OD professional?"

"No."

"Then how does he know what needs to be done?"

"He doesn't."

"It sounds like you don't really do Organization Development work here."

"Well, that's a matter of opinion. People who do well here don't question these things."

"How can you do OD work without questioning things? That's fundamental to uncovering problems."

Sherman's face became tense; he locked his jaw as he shot back his response, "That's how we do OD here, and if we didn't do it this way, this department wouldn't exist! They wouldn't have us!"

Ally knew she was wasting her time. She had no intention of applying for the position, so she graciously ended the conversation.

Let Me Tell You a Story

Foreign dignitaries visited a U.S. company to learn about its operations. Guthrie, a Director, guided one of the dignitaries on tours of several operations centers. He asked two of the managers in his organization, Tim and Kari, to accompany him and explain the operations at one site. Guthrie drove the car on the way to the centers. The visitor sat in the front passenger seat and Tim and Kari sat in the back seat. As they were riding, the visitor asked Guthrie,

"How are people promoted in your company?"

Guthrie grinned as he responded, "Let me tell you a story: I once accepted a manager for an assignment in my department as a favor to a colleague. This manager was being considered for advancement to the top levels of the organization. The purpose of this assignment was for him to become familiar with another department's operations…"

"Is that how it's usually done?"

"Yes, but only for those who are targeted for upper level positions. Anyway, I didn't like this guy from the first day I met him, but I already agreed to the arrangement so I was stuck with him."

"Were you supposed to promote him?"

"No, I was supposed to evaluate his potential. So I assigned him to a critical project. The guy took control and began interpreting policy. We'd have these one-on-one meetings and he'd tell me what he'd been up to. One day I told him I disagreed with one of his decisions. He should have said 'Yes, sir' and gone out and reversed his decision; instead, he asked me to explain why. I let his decision stand, but that was the last time he got a critical assignment in my department. When I gave my evaluation to my colleague, I told him I didn't see this manager's potential for promotion."

Guthrie then grinned from ear-to-ear, and said, "That was seven years ago and, to this day, that guy has not been promoted—and he probably never will be. That's the way it's done here."

Tim and Kari glanced at each other with widened eyes. The next day, Tim asked Kari, "What did you think of that story Guthrie told about promoting people in our company?"

"I can't believe he told that story in front of us! But what an eye-opener! I know the guy he was talking about—he's one of the best managers in the company. I always wondered why he didn't get ahead."

"Yeah, I wondered too; so much for good work. I'd always heard rumors, but now I guess we know for sure why some of these duds we have for managers got their jobs."

"Yes, sir; yes, sir!"

Everywhere that Perry Went, Sam was Sure to Go

Perry popped into Deana's office and said, "Deana, I want to introduce you to Sam. I just interviewed him, and he's going to be joining our department in two weeks."

"Hi, Sam. Nice to meet you. What are you going to be doing?"

"It's administrative."

"Oh, great! We've been needing a coordinator. Have you done this kind of work before?"

Perry interjected, "Sam's not going to be our coordinator."

"Oh, sorry. What's he going to do?"

Perry responded, "Well, it's not all worked out yet, but there are a lot of things I need help with."

"Oh, okay." "Welcome Sam! I'm looking forward to working with you."

"Thanks. I'm looking forward to working with you, too."

During Sam's first week on the job, Perry said to Deana, "I'd like you to invite Sam to the review meeting for your new course today so he can learn about the kinds of things we do here."

During the meeting, Sam challenged Deana's approach several times. At one point he said, "No, that's wrong. You should include these topics in that lesson…"

Confused about Sam's role and his apparent lack of knowledge, Deana asked, "Are you an Instructional Designer?"

"No, but I've spent a lot of time around training and I know that this is the way it's done."

"Are you going to be developing courses here?"

"No."

"Maybe we should talk about this later. Can you stick around after the meeting?"

"Sure."

When the meeting was over, Deana said, "I'd like to get to know you a little better and understand how we're going to be working together."

"Oh, thanks, that's a great idea! Well, I used to work with Perry in my last job before he came here. He's been my mentor—I really admire him and have learned a lot from him. I was so glad that he called me and offered me this position."

"What are you going to be doing?"

"Well, there's lots of stuff he wants me to get involved with, and I'm going to help you guys out any way I can."

Several other meetings followed. Each time, Deana explained different aspects of the work to Sam—never certain what his job was. She learned that Sam was a high-school graduate who had held administrative and secretarial positions in the past, and that he had just started to attend college on a part-time basis. Communicating with him was difficult. He had trouble saying what he meant and wrote unclear, incomplete sentences. Deana began to teach him some of the underlying principles of her profession so he would understand the reasons why training programs were written as they were. His lack of education made it difficult for him to grasp some of the behavioral and learning concepts yet he tried to direct Deana's work.

Deana began to notice that after every meeting with Sam, Perry would call her and tell her to include or exclude things in her courses that he couldn't have known about without having spoken to Sam. The things he told her to include were the very suggestions Sam had made—suggestions that were inappropriate.

Two months later, Perry took a medical leave of absence. He informed everyone in the company to contact Sam in his absence for assistance with anything in the department. Sam contacted Perry daily while he was on leave, responded to all of his messages and correspondence, and filtered all information to and from Deana and the other managers in the department.

What Propagator Bosses Want from You

Propagator Bosses want you to be their student, disciple, collaborator, co-conspirator, and they want you to help them climb the career ladder. They want you to be a "blank slate" with regard to the functions that they oversee so that they can "mold" you into the type of employee they want you to be. They want you to take them at their word and follow their explicit and precise instructions in everything you do without questioning their intentions or methods, even when you sense that those methods are wrong. They want you to admire them for their knowledge and their willingness to "take you under their wing" and "develop" you.

Propagator Bosses want you to be a quick-learner and to be politically astute. They want you to be their "eyes and ears" when they are not present. They want you to report to them about what others are doing in the organization so that they can outperform them. Propagator Bosses want you to attend meetings as a "spy" on their behalf even though you have no legitimate reason to be at those meetings. They want you to cover their back and defend what they do whenever they are mentioned by others. They want you to identify significant projects in which others are engaged so they can become involved with those projects. If they are able to do so, they want you to help them take over those projects. If they are unable to take control, they want you to help them find a way to participate and, at the very least, share the recognition.

Propagator Bosses want you to help them put a spin on information so that it helps them look good in the eyes of their management. They want you to prepare elaborate reports and presentations for them that are skewed to demonstrate their effectiveness as a manager. They want you to help them take credit for the work of their peers in other departments or at least to gain some of the credit as "a good team player." They want you to help them acquire functions in their department that give them more power within the organization.

Reporting to a Propagator Boss

Reporting to a Propagator Boss is like being a devoted cheerleader. To get along with your Propagator Boss you must defer to her or him as though your boss is royalty and you are a loyal subject. You must follow blindly and do as you are told. You must disengage from your morals and ethics and forget about the concept of fairness. You must see your workplace as a game board in which the object is for your boss to win. You must regard other participants in this "game" as nuisances who have the potential to block you and your boss from winning. If there are "rules" in the game, then you must find a way to get around those rules in order to "win." You must become comfortable with cheating to get ahead and you must become skilled at covering up your tactics.

People who are highly competitive, who need someone to direct them, who are willing to hold a "second place" position and who are unrestrained by ethics can survive in this type of reporting relationship with the least amount of negative stress. Once you have earned the trust of a Propagator Boss and have become a mentee, he or she will share political strategies with you for advancing your career.

If you are new to your organization, you may be surprised that your Propagator Boss hired you because of your lack of specific qualifications. You would not have been hired by your Propagator Boss unless you demonstrated your willingness to work as stated in the previous paragraph. If those attributes accurately describe you, then it is likely that you will become a mentee and advance quickly along with your boss—as long as you continue to be your boss's loyal student and disciple.

If you are highly competent in your field and the attributes stated above do not accurately describe you, then your propagator boss either hired you by mistake or acquired you through some transaction in which he or she had no choice. You will be disregarded by your Propagator Boss and assigned to menial tasks. Your Propagator Boss will cut you off when you speak, as if saying: "You can't possibly have anything important to say" or "You are not smart enough to be of value to me in any way." You will be expected to do your job quietly without recognition or acknowledgement for your efforts, and to stay out of your boss's way. If you work on your boss's pet projects, he or she will tell you exactly what to do. If you do not obey, you will be reassigned to insignificant projects and one of your boss's mentees or a contractor or consultant hired by your boss will take over your work. To recapture your boss's attention, you will have to identify an opportunity for your boss to get into the limelight and get your boss involved.

The Propagator Boss Survival Quiz

Examine your relationship with your Propagator Boss objectively in this "True-or-False" quiz:

Statement:	T	F
1. You do not want to understand the reasons why things are done in a certain way.		
2. You want specific, explicit and detailed directions from your boss.		
3. You do not mind working with unqualified contractors, consultants or vendors; or taking direction from them when your boss instructs you to do so.		
4. You do not want to develop expertise in a professional discipline; you are satisfied with being a generalist.		
5. You believe "it's only a job" and you are willing to do it however your boss wants you to do it.		
6. You want your boss to be your mentor.		
7. Your relationship with your boss is more important to you than the work, the organization or the organization's customers or other stakeholders.		
8. You are willing to do whatever it takes to achieve higher-level positions.		

If you responded "<u>True</u>" to five or more of these statements, there is a good chance that you might survive reporting to your Propagator Boss without experiencing much negative stress—as long as you continue to report to this boss.

If you responded "<u>False</u>" to four or more of these statements, then you are already negatively impacted in your current position.

Strategies for Surviving Your Propagator Boss

If you report to a Propagator Boss and you responded "False" to half of the statements in the Survival Quiz, then transferring or leaving the organization are your best options. Surviving this type of boss involves getting as far away from her or him as you can and doing work that does not come into contact with this boss or her or his mentees, contractors and consultants.

Plan to transfer as soon as you realize that your boss is not informing you about what is going on in the organization. Locate a position in a department with which your Propagator Boss has no interaction or influence. When making your transfer request, tell you boss that the job you are interested in is a better match for your skills. Emphasize that you will be a more valuable employee to the organization in another position. Downplay your competence and do not mention any dissatisfaction with your current situation.

Be relaxed when you have this conversation; practice with someone else before you approach your boss. Your boss will try to read into your request to determine if you might be a threat in any way; being tense might indicate to your boss that you are displeased with her or him.

While working toward obtaining a new position, consider using these tactics for getting along with your Propagator Boss:

- Keep in mind that your Propagator Boss is trying to get promoted; do whatever you can to help.
- Pretend to be your Propagator Boss's student.

- Always obtain and follow your boss's explicit and precise instructions before acting.

If transferring to another department with which your boss has no association is not a viable option, then consider leaving the organization. Chapter 14, *Basic Bad-Boss Survival Strategies,* provides additional advice for choosing to leave.

If you responded "True" to five or more of the statements in the Propagator Boss Survival Quiz, then your success depends on your relationship to your boss and you have become her or his co-collaborator. You may survive as long as your boss is able to win the favor of his or her managers. Be aware of a major reorganization in your organization. If your boss cannot easily influence the new management, you will both be at risk of losing your jobs.

Strategies that Won't Work

Your Propagator Boss will be threatened if you question her or his intentions and will strike out at you in response, so it is best not to mention your concerns. Your Propagator Boss is also uninterested in your job-satisfaction or dissatisfaction, and any attempt to discuss this matter is a nuisance that diverts your boss from the goal of climbing the ladder-of-success. Furthermore, your boss has most likely positioned herself or himself with upper-level managers so favorably that he or she is respected by them. This will make it difficult or impossible for you to be taken seriously if you escalate your concerns.

Interview Strategies

What to listen for:

- *We do things differently here.*
- *This company has a way of doing things that's probably a lot different from what you're used to.*
- *If you take this job, you'll have to learn to do things my way.*

When you hear these statements, ask questions such as:

- How are the ways you do things here different from what they do in other organizations?
- Why is it so different here?
- How did you develop your methods?

Responses that do not completely answer your questions indicate that the manager you are interviewing may be a Propagator Boss.

Accepting the Consequences of Staying

If you are one of your boss's mentees, then you must continue to dote on her or him. As soon as you try to become independent, you will fall out of favor with your boss, be assigned to insignificant projects and be given poor performance reviews. Your boss will block your attempts to work anywhere else in the organization by falsely giving bad reports of your performance to any manager who considers hiring you.

If you *must* remain, or if you choose to remain in a reporting relationship with a Propagator Boss but you are *not* one of your boss's mentees, then be prepared to be disregarded and unappreciated. You will not get satisfaction from your current job. Find other outlets to express your talents and receive recognition and appreciation. Consider volunteer work or a part-time job at an organization that appreciates your skills and abilities. If you are so stressed by your association with your Propagator Boss that you are unable to seek other outlets, consider counseling. Refer to the Appendix: *Where to Find Help*, for additional information.

7: THE PLAYER

"It's my department and I'll do the jobs I like!"

How to Recognize a Player Boss

"What a good idea! I like this form you came up with! Only two weeks on the job and already you're helping us get us organized!"

"Thanks! I'm glad you think it'll help."

"It sure will! Did you make this in Excel?"

"Yes, I did."

"I love to make forms in Excel! Next time you get an idea to do something like this, just tell me about it and I'll make it up, okay?

"Uh, okay." Alisha was puzzled: *Why would my boss want to spend time making up administrative forms?*

Player Bosses disregard their management responsibilities while they perform the jobs of the employees who report to them. Their department is their sandbox and they are like misbehaving children who take toys and things away from others. They want authority but they do not want the responsibility of managing people, projects, or a department. Instead, they want to perform the hands-on work of the employees who report to them. They use their authority to do whatever jobs they want to do, whether or not they are qualified.

Player Bosses agree to manage a department when they accept their managerial position, but what they really want is the opportunity to perform the technical work in that department. Player Bosses perform only the interesting parts of the jobs assigned to the people who report to them. They leave the mundane tasks for their employees to complete or to correct after they have made mistakes.

Some Player Bosses are very good at performing the work of the people who report to them, particularly those who once worked at that job and enjoyed it. Other Player Bosses are unqualified for the technical jobs in the department they are supposed to manage, but they try to do them anyway. They assume they are smarter than the people who report to them just because they are the boss, and that being smarter makes them able to perform the work of the specialists who report to them—even though they lack the necessary training.

People who become Player Bosses are usually those who never chose the profession they are working in now, but stumbled across it later in their career and found it interesting. When they finally find the work that interests them, Player Bosses often already hold a higher level position than that work requires.

Listen for these statements:

- "I'll do that part…"
- "I'll do the tough parts so that we can get done quickly…"
- "This might be too difficult for you, so I'll handle it…"
- "Pick up where I left off…"
- "People should have fun at work…"
- "Wouldn't it be fun to…?"

These statements signal that the person speaking is likely to be a Player Boss. Managers who assign projects to you but tell you that they will do some of the work are trying to do your job while ignoring their management duties.

Let the last expression in this list: "Wouldn't it be fun to…?" be an alarm when you hear it; it can be a strong signal that the Player Boss does not know the underlying principles of the profession or discipline. Player Bosses want to try different techniques without knowing the reasons why those techniques must or must not be performed, and without being aware of the potentially negative consequences. Player Bosses do your work to provide for entertainment rather than to satisfy the needs of the organization or its customers or recipients.

Statements about "having fun at work" hint at the Player Boss's greater interest in wanting to be entertained. The statement: "have fun at work" is contradictory to the result of work. Think about this for a moment: if you wanted to have fun, would you go to work? Most likely, you would engage in some recreational activity to have fun. Fun is the result of play. The result of work, especially good work, is <u>satisfaction</u> (the result of bad work is <u>dis</u>satisfaction). If you enjoy your work, you probably do so because it provides you with a sense of satisfaction or accomplishment. Enjoyment is satisfying and satisfaction lasts for a long while, but fun is fleeting and short-lived; fun and satisfaction are two very different experiences. People who work in professional sports are not "playing" to have "fun" when they are at work; they work in the entertainment field—they entertain others to earn money. Professional athletes get satisfaction from their work when they win because by doing so they please their fans (customers) and their managers, as well as themselves. When they lose, they have done their job—they may feel dissatisfied with not having won, but, still, they have fulfilled their purpose and entertained their fans—who will come to see them work again (something your organization's "customers" are unlikely to do if you fail them). When professional athletes go out to have fun, they do not usually engage in the "game" of their profession—they do something unrelated to their work that is recreational for them. Player Bosses do your job for recreation, and they are being paid at a higher salary level than you for work they are not doing.

Player Bosses may pretend they are helping you so they can take your projects away from you. They preface their "takeover" with phrases such as: "Let me pitch in and help you with this." They act as though they're making a great sacrifice by doing your job in order to "help" you or the organization or its customers. They come across as though they are struggling with the extra workload of your job. This is a ploy to obtain sympathy from you while manipulating you into surrendering your responsibilities to them—work they would rather do. They ignore their own responsibilities while doing your job at their salary level.

Player bosses typically integrate their personal lives with their professional lives. They may open up their homes for work-related events. Their friends are almost exclusively work associates. They consider as "friends" those people who report to them and express their praise and admiration for the boss. This "friendship" is one-sided, however. It is all "taking" and no "giving." Player Bosses behave as though they believe you are indebted to them for employing you and obliged to let them have fun doing whatever jobs they'd like to do.

Player Boss Examples

Because I Can

Gerald positioned himself as an expert in the field of Human Resource Development to get his job as head of the training department. His Ph.D. in an academic discipline did not qualify him to oversee workplace training, yet he convinced the executives in his large company that it did.

But Gerald didn't really want to be the boss; he didn't want to oversee the managers of the employees who developed training—he wanted to develop the training himself, even though he didn't know how. He overrode the authority of the managers who reported to him and performed the work that should have been done by the employees who reported to those managers. When the managers objected to his methods, he pacified them by hiring Byron, a Performance Management Consultant who specialized in Instructional Design, to advise them about appropriate methods. Gerald thought he was clever enough to fool Byron into justifying his behavior.

During Byron's first week on the job, Gerald said,

"I'd like you to attend one of the planning sessions for a course I'm designing."

"Sure. What do you want me to contribute to your session?"

"Just watch. This is an interesting course and I thought it would be good for you to see some of the things we're trying to accomplish here."

"Okay, I'll be there."

Gerald and two of the managers who report to him were present. Byron was surprised that no Course Developers participated in this course development project. He watched as Gerald giggled and introduced random suggestions in a child-like voice. For example, at one point Gerald said,

"Ooh, ooh! I have a good idea! Wouldn't this be fun…we'll put the student trainers [the course participants] in an exercise where their practice audience gives them nothing but resistance! We'll have the managers of our department act as the practice audience and no matter what the participants do, the practice audience will be obnoxious! Then we'll observe how these student trainers handle it. What do you think?"

The managers shook their heads up and down as they laughed. They suggested a few obnoxious things the practice audience could act out and laughed heartily at how funny it would be to watch. Byron continued to observe silently, as he had been instructed, until Gerald asked,

"What do you think about this exercise, Byron?"

"It's hard for me to comment without knowing what lesson you are teaching before this exercise. It looks like I've come in at the middle of your planning session, so I don't know what you've already designed."

"We haven't designed *anything* yet; this is only our second meeting. We're just coming up with some exercises that we think'll be fun."

"I don't see how you can design an exercise before you determine the objectives of the course and the skills you plan to teach. You *are* going to teach the student trainers how to handle these situations before you introduce this exercise, aren't you?"

"Oh, no, that wouldn't be any fun! I like to watch what people do in awkward situations! We'll start the course this way and then debrief them so they'll get the learning at the end."

"It sounds like you're setting them up to fail *and* to be humiliated. That approach can have a damaging psychological and sociological impact on adult learners."

Gerald snapped back, "What would you do, Byron?"

"Set them up to succeed."

"No! They won't learn anything that way! I know what I'm doing!"

Gerald resumed his activity and ignored Byron for the remainder of the meeting. Byron observed quietly. After the meeting, Gerald said to Byron privately,

"I'd like your feedback. How do you think that went?"

Byron responded with a question of his own, "I don't understand something. Why are *you* working at this level of detail, doing the work of the employees who hold positions two levels below yours?"

Gerald squinted, forced a broad, flat smile, tilted his head to the right, and said:

"Because I like to play, and I'm the Boss, so I can."

I'm so Good at Your Job

Some Player Bosses actually compete with the employees who report to them. Delia encountered one at her new luxury-product sales job. She attended an employee orientation meeting during her first day on the job. Her new boss, Phil, said to her and the one other newly hired sales employee,

"My closing ratio is 70%—I close the sale with seven of every ten potential customers I meet with. But all the people I've hired to work in this position have only been able to achieve a 40% closing ratio."

Delia said, "Wow, that's a big difference. Considering that this is a commission-only job, 40% means earnings on less than half the time spent selling. What closing ratio do you expect us to meet?"

"I think you'll start out at around 40%, but you should get to 70% in about a month or two.

"But if the others are only selling at a 40% rate, what makes you think it will be different for us?"

"I'm going to spend these next two weeks training you. You'll get a salary while you're learning. I haven't done this with the other sales people—they've learned as they went along."

"Will we be able to meet some of the other sales people during these two weeks and ask them questions?"

"No, that won't be possible."

"Why not?"

"Because you're the only two sales people I have."

"Where's the rest of the sales staff?"

"You're it. That's why I'm having this meeting with you. I need to get you up to speed quickly."

"How long have you been the manager here?"

"I worked at headquarters in a staff job for six years. I got interested in running this branch when the previous manager retired. When I saw how much this region was growing I thought there was a great opportunity here. I've had this branch for four years now and I've quadrupled the sales that the previous manager was getting."

"Wow! That's great, and it sounds very encouraging. How many sales people have worked here over the last three years?"

"Oh, they've come and gone. Let's see, there's been eight of them."

"Why is turnover so high?"

"They just didn't have what it takes to be good sales people. It's easy for *me* to make 70%; I guess I just have a knack for selling."

"What's the longest anyone has stayed in this job?"

"Six months."

Delia began to worry: *Why has no one lasted more than six months in this job? Why does Phil have a sales ratio at all—how can he manage the branch and still outsell all the people who report to him?* She asked,

"How are you able to sell at such a high rate and still manage the branch?"

"At times like this, when there's no sales staff, I do the selling. Now that you're here, I'll be able to devote my time to managing the business."

Two months later, Delia and her colleague each had a 40% closing ratio while Phil maintained a 70% ratio. Phil took all the sales leads from the most affluent part of the region. Delia discovered that it was much easier to sell their high-end luxury products in that market on the few occasions she was given leads in that territory because Phil was too busy to handle them.

That Job Looks Like More Fun

Charlene had just gotten promoted to the position of Sales Vice President for a division of a large, national company. Her new boss assigned her to solve several problems, one of which was the lack of adequate sales training for entry and mid-level sales employees. She had no background in training, so Charlene hired Theo into the position of Director of Training and charged him with creating and managing a Sales Training Department:

"It's absolute chaos out in the field. The branch managers hire new people to handle walk-in sales and send them to headquarters to attend a two-week class that's been around for years. After the training, these new people still have no idea what to do back on the job. Once they spend a few months inside at their branch office, we assign accounts to them and send them out to develop business. I need you to figure out what these people need and find a way to get them up to speed as quickly as possible. This is your area—it's your opportunity to create a department just the way you think it should be. Hire the people you need and get the programs we need in place quickly. Just keep me posted."

Theo purchased a training program that was ideal for the traveling sales staff and told Charlene about it:

"The vendor is conducting a train-the-trainer session at our facility next week. I'm going to attend along with the new trainers I hired to deliver this course across the country. Would you like to sit in on the session to become familiar with my new people and the new course material?"

"Yes. That sounds like a good idea."

After the attending that session, Theo had his staff schedule classes. A week later, he got a call from one of the Branch Managers:

"…You booked my people to attend two different classes at the same time! No one told me this second class was available and no one asked me who I wanted to send—you just assigned my people to attend without my knowledge, and they're not even available—they have meetings with clients! What to hell's going on?"

"Whoa—wait a minute! There's only one class and we don't assign your people to attend. I personally sent you a letter announcing this class and asked you if you wanted to send anyone. We signed up the people whose names were on your list. There is no other class that week."

"Well they just got notice that they're attending another one during the same week!"

"Who sent the notice?"

"It's signed by your boss, Charlene."

"What? I don't know anything about it. Let me look into this and get back to you."

Charlene wasn't available, so Theo asked her secretary if she was aware of any meetings Charlene had scheduled during that week. Her secretary said:

"Oh, yes, I know what that is. Charlene asked me to set up sales-training classes in the regions. It's taking up all my time to do this. I've got to book conference rooms at hotels, and make transportation and lodging arrangements for her, too."

Theo questioned Charlene as soon as she got back. Charlene explained:

"I've got to meet with all these people anyway. Don't you think it'll be inspiring to these new people to have their Vice President train them?"

Charlene had taken over Theo's job and the job of the schedulers and trainers who report to her and never told her what he was doing.

What Player Bosses Want from You

Player Bosses want you to praise them. Think of a child who keeps asking: "I'm a good boy (or girl), aren't I?" This is your Player Boss. Player Bosses behave as though they are still trying to obtain the approval of one or both of their parents. You are expected to play a role similar to that of an approving "parent" while you allow your Player Boss to dominate you. There is a fine line you must not cross in this relationship. You have the power to trigger a Player Boss's insecurities with the slightest indication of your disapproval, and Player Bosses work diligently to keep you in check and not allow that to happen. They resent that you have this power yet, at the same time, they give you the power to praise them. They look to you for encouragement and are very sensitive to your body language and vocal inflections. They may seem paranoid and they are inclined to perceive anything you say or do negatively unless it is accompanied by enthusiasm in your voice and gestures with credits to them for your excitement. You cannot laud enough praise on these bosses; they seem to need adulation almost as much as they need oxygen, regardless of their level in the organization's hierarchy.

Player Bosses want you to act as though you are their friend and buddy—a play-pal in their sandbox—but they want you to always let them win at whatever "game" they are playing with you. They want you tell them they are "right" and "brilliant" even when they are "wrong" and "ignorant." They want you to let them take the lead role in your projects, or at least give them credit for being the "brains" behind your projects. They want you to admire their willingness to "pitch in and lend a hand" with the technical work.

Player Bosses want you to pretend that they know more than you know about your specialization when they do not. They do not want you to try to "explain" things to them or to "teach" them anything—they see these gestures as threats: criticism, expressions of disapproval, and/or attempts to dominate them, rather than as helpful and cooperative attempts to collaborate with them. There is no collaboration with Player Bosses—they reign supreme and they want you to play the role of their loyal subject.

Reporting to a Player Boss

Reporting to a Player Boss is like playing with a manipulative and mean child; a child who has the will and the ability to hurt you whenever he or she wants something you have or suspects that you are better than her or him or more advantaged in any way. Player Bosses interpret questions about their behavior as challenges and expressions of disapproval. Questions about their behavior trigger their wrath. Player Bosses use the power assigned to them to suppress or quash employees who report to them and who question their actions.

When Player Bosses give you advice, they are likely to quote or paraphrase a parent who was particularly harsh, distant, or disapproving toward them. This advice almost always carries with it a derogatory inference, such as: "My father always told me to come down off my high horse because I can be wrong, too" or "My mother always said that self praise has a bad aroma."

Employees who are marginally competent and willing to do menial tasks routinely, or who have accepted their job as an interim position, or who are using their position as a stepping stone to seize a better opportunity at another organization in the near future, can survive in this type of reporting relationship with the least amount of negative stress.

If you are new to your organization, then you may be taken aback by your boss's "friendliness" and willingness to "help" you do your job. You are being tested to determine how far and for how long you will let your boss go on performing your duties, and how much "appreciation" you will show her or him for doing your job for you. When you ask for a chance to do your job on your own, you will see a dramatic shift in your Player Boss's attitude toward you— a very unfavorable shift.

If you are competent and better equipped to perform your job than your Player Boss, you will become frustrated in your work. To survive with a minimum of negative consequences, you must be willing to sacrifice the purpose and goals of your organization and the needs of its customers or recipients to your Player Boss's whimsy. Your attempts to inform or educate your boss will backfire on you—they will be perceived negatively and your Player Boss will falsely accuse you of incompetence, regardless of the quality of your work, the extent of your experience, or the validity of your credentials. These accusations will feel particularly harsh because your Player Boss is not qualified to assess your performance adequately or accurately. If you question your Player Boss's actions or reasoning, he or she will banish you from her or his "in-group" or "circle-of-friends" and will not speak to you unless it is absolutely necessary to do so. Your Player Boss will then give you insignificant assignments or no assignments at all. He or she will instruct your work associates that they are not to deal directly with you about any work issues and that they are to see her or him about any matter that involves you.

The Player Boss Survival Quiz

Examine your relationship with your Player objectively in this "True-or-False" quiz:

Statement:	T	F
1. It is okay with you that your boss competes with you on the job.		
2. You do not mind that your boss uses organizational information to compete with rather than sharing that information.		
3. You do not mind doing only those parts of your job that require minimal skill or are tedious and mundane.		
4. You do not mind being disregarded when you make suggestions.		
5. You do not mind being told that you are "wrong" when you are "right."		
6. You do not mind "cleaning up" after your boss when he or she makes mistakes while doing your job.		
7. You are working in your job just so that you can qualify for a similar position at another organization.		
8. You enjoy watching your boss do things incorrectly or that are potentially harmful.		

If you responded "True" to most of these statements, then there is a good chance that you might survive reporting to a Player Boss without experiencing undesirable consequences.

If you responded "False" to two or more of these statements, then it is very likely that you will be negatively impacted in your current position.

Strategies for Surviving Your Player Boss

If you report to a Player Boss and you responded "False" to any of the statements in the Survival Quiz, then leaving the organization is probably your best option. A transfer might work for you if your organization has another department that requires your skills and expertise, has an opening, and is managed by a boss who is not described in this book. Your Player Boss will be unhappy and offended by your decision to leave, so do not give notice more than two weeks before the date on which you plan to leave. Player Bosses do not like staffing vacant positions—that takes away from their "playtime." It is also difficult for your Player Boss to staff positions in her or his department because it is difficult to find and hire competent people who will tolerate her or his behavior. This boss will not be a good reference for you, so make your move as soon as your realize that you are not going to have the opportunity to perform the job you were hired to do. Rely on former managers for references and do not include this job in your resume if you leave within five months of being hired.

While you are planning your move, consider these interim strategies:

- You can position yourself well with a Player Boss by pretending to be a "friend" or "buddy."

- Player Bosses like to hear that they are "right" and "brilliant" even when they are "wrong" and "ignorant."

- It's better to compliment a Player Boss for "pitching in and helping" when he or she is interfering than to ask for autonomy.

- Accept that you will spend a great deal of time cleaning up after a Player Boss—he or she will frequently create chaos with your projects.

Strategies that Won't Work

Your Player Boss most likely reports to a higher-level manager who has limited or no knowledge of your technical specialization, and does not hold your boss accountable for management responsibilities. Your Player Boss has most likely convinced her or his manager that detailed involvement in your work is an effective management style for the type of work that is performed in the department. If so, then higher-level managers most likely see your boss as someone who "goes above and beyond the call of duty" by stepping in and "lending a hand" to the technical work performed in your department, and your boss is probably being rewarded for doing your job. For these reasons, you will have little credibility if you try to escalate your concerns.

Talking with your boss and requesting that he or she allow you to perform your job entirely on your own without interference will not work either. Player Bosses may respond to such a request by saying: "Your job is whatever I tell you it is—you don't decide what work you get to do here; that's my decision!" From your boss's perspective, you are there just to sweep up the sand that falls out of the sandbox while your boss is playing. Your boss will not give up the work he or she wants to do so you can have a fulfilling career—even if that work is in your job description—doing so would render your boss's days at work unfulfilling.

Interview Strategies

What to listen for:

- *I'm a hands-on manager.*
- *I often pitch in to help get the job done.*

If you hear statements like these, ask questions such as:

- How much autonomy will I have in this job?
- How does your work differ from mine in this position?
- Do you see a clear separation of boundaries between your responsibilities and the responsibilities of this position?
- Have you ever taken over a project from one of your employees? If so, what happened?

If the manager interviewing you indicates that there are no clear boundaries, or that he or she likes to collaborate about the work, you may be interviewing with a Player Boss.

Accepting the Consequences of Staying

If you are competent at your job, and if you choose to continue to report to a Player Boss even though you responded "False" to two or more questions in the Survival Quiz, then be prepared to lower your standards. Get comfortable with the idea of supporting your boss's poor-quality work, and recognize that it is your decision to do so. Advice cautioning you to "do the best job you can" is useless—you cannot do the best job you are capable of doing if a Player Boss wants to dabble in your job, and there is little or no support available to you. Through counseling, you are likely to discover that you must put this experience behind you to maintain your sense of self-esteem and to minimize the negative stress in your life.

If you <u>must</u> remain in a reporting relationship with a Player Boss, consider the situation to be temporary and begin doing whatever is necessary to make a move as soon as possible. Knowing that you are taking steps toward improving your situation can help you to tolerate your Player Boss for a little while. As a stress reliever, write resignation letters frequently, but do not submit them (write them at home—not at work). Set a goal for the date on which you will submit your actual resignation. And above all else, once you have found other employment, stick to your decision to move on even if you receive a counter offer from your current employer. Your situation will not improve at your current workplace.

8: THE BULLY

"It's such fun to see you squirm!"

How to Recognize a Bully Boss

Merta conducted a study during the first three weeks on her new job, so she didn't get to know her knew new boss or colleagues very well. As she finalized her report for the presentation she was going to make to her Director and colleagues, she heard singing outside her office:

"Merta's in the hot seat…Merta's in the hot seat."

The tune was familiar—she had heard children sing it when they chided each other, saying "nah-nah, nah-nah, nah-nah," but these were her colleagues—middle-level managers. She invited them into her office, but they stopped at the doorway and wouldn't come in.

"What's all this singing all about?" she asked.

"Today's your first meeting; you're making your first presentation—it's your turn in the hot seat."

"What do you mean?"

"You'll see."

"Is there something I should know about before this meeting?"

"You'll find out soon enough."

As Merta presented her findings, her new boss shot questions at her, interrupting every sentence she spoke, snapping,

"Wait a minute, this isn't the format we use here, redo this before you distribute it…Did you get comments from people at every skill level?… Where's the support for this?…Are you sure this is right?…How did you determine this?…What were they doing?…Why did they say that?…Are you sure you got it right?"

118

When one of Merta's colleagues spoke up to lend support, the Director's face turned red as she yelled, "You keep out of this! I'll determine how we're going to interpret this report!" The Director continued to holler in a red-faced frenzy as she fired more questions at Merta.

After the meeting, Merta's singing colleagues congratulated her, saying, "You passed with flying colors!" "You handled it very well!" "You never lost your composure—that's good!" "You'll do well here."

Merta asked, "Is it always like this?

"This was your first time. Everyone goes through it."

"When does it stop?"

"It depends."

Bully Bosses try to intimidate the people who report to them. They insult, taunt, harass, and threaten employees. They snap, shout, ridicule, and/or curse at them. While abusing people, both verbally and psychologically, Bully Bosses have that cat-that-swallowed-the-canary, satirical expression on their faces. They appear to be out of control while attacking, but they are very much in control and keenly aware of the emotional reactions of the people around them. A Bully Boss's rage may be seen as an implied physical threat, but it does not usually escalate to physical violence.

To the people who report to them, Bully Bosses appear to have a personality disorder—similar to multiple personality disorder, but different in that the switch between personalities is completely within their control. As obnoxious as they can be with the people over whom they have some degree of authority, Bully Bosses are pussycats with their superiors. They are very adept at convincing their managers that they are mild-mannered, respectful and submissive people. The managers to whom Bully Bosses report rarely, if ever, suspect or believe that Bully Bosses are capable of behaving in the way that they do with their employees. Their managers are usually very pleased with Bully Bosses because Bully

119

Bosses appear to be very capable of "getting results" from the people who report to them.

Bully Bosses make it very clear to people positioned below them in the hierarchy that they want to get their way. They become extremely agitated when someone else's idea gets more attention than their own suggestion. They want to win and they want you to lose. They play "dirty" so they can win. It is not enough for Bully Bosses to just get their way; they want to strip you of your dignity and power in every transaction they have with you; they want you to be left with an unsatisfactory outcome. Bully Bosses do not compromise—as they see it, compromising is losing because you will have obtained an acceptable outcome and they want you to be disappointed and dissatisfied.

Bully Bosses are keen observers of people and they are very good at reading body language. They assess everyone they come in contact with as a potential target for their hostility by looking for signs of submission and weakness. Bully Bosses see cooperation, collaboration and consideration as signs of weakness—those characteristics that are at the root of civility and workplace effectiveness are the attributes that Bully Bosses seek when looking for their prey. Bully Bosses are quick to take advantage of those who attempt to do the "right thing" and work effectively with other people to accomplish the organization's goals. They consider people with that kind of integrity to be easy prey whom they can beat with a minimum of effort and with a few unfair or dishonest tactics. Winning is the primary objective of Bully Bosses—personally winning at anything at all is of utmost importance to them, regardless of the cost to others and to the organization that employs them.

Bully Bosses are unrelenting with their "targets" and want to loom victorious over them. They continually criticize their targets in an attempt to chip away at their self-esteem. They may imply threats or they may even blatantly threaten their targets with undeserved job loss, poor ratings, and/or damage to their reputations. They place unreasonable demands on targets and set unrealistic objectives for them. As a result, their targets can only be assessed as having performed poorly when measured according to arbitrarily-set "standards" constructed by the Bully Boss. Bully Bosses also withhold important information and resources from their targets to cause them to perform poorly. They get the target's co-workers to make false accusations against the target to justify their behavior. Even when their targets do exceedingly-good work, Bully Bosses either raise doubts about that work, or tear it apart with false critiques about its accuracy, comprehensiveness and/or relevance.

Bully Bosses surround themselves with work associates who boost their ego. They like to associate with people who are aggressive with other associates, or at least assertive, but who willingly subordinate themselves to the Bully Boss. This includes both the employees who report to them and the external contractors, consultants and vendors they hire to work in their organization. These associates become the Bully Boss's personal circle of "friends" outside of the workplace; however, these people are not genuine friends of the Bully Boss. Aggressive and assertive people who subordinate themselves to Bully Bosses do so only because they receive benefits from their association with the Bully Boss— benefits which they could not obtain as easily without their alliance with the Bully Boss. These benefits usually include undeserved compensation and special privileges not granted to others. As long as Bully Bosses provide these benefits, their "friends" stick around.

Listen for name-calling, frequent use of profanity, and phrases similar to these:

- "You think you're pretty smart, don't you…?"
- "What makes you think you know so much…?"
- "Just because you have *(fill in the blank)* doesn't mean you can *(fill in the blank)*."
- "I'm *your* boss…"
- "*I'm* the boss around here…"
- "Your work is good only if *I say* it's good…"

- "You're nothing around here without me…"
- "Can't you follow simple instructions?"
- "You'll do what I say…"

Managers who resort to using phrases like these are most likely Bully Bosses. They intend to be abrupt and offensive, and to trigger feelings of weakness and insecurity in you. Statements that question, challenge or criticize your knowledge, skills and character are intended to challenge your confidence and make you back off. The use of these critical and/or antagonistic statements indicates that the Bully Boss senses he or she is "losing" and you are "winning."

When Bully Bosses state the obvious by telling you that they are "the boss," they are implying that they want to have their way; that they want to "win" regardless of whether they are right or wrong. These statements are the Bully Boss's declaration of war with you—a war that has a predetermined outcome—the Bully Boss will win by using any tactic necessary to do so.

When you make a good point, perform a job well without crediting your Bully Boss for the outcome, or perform a job well without directly following your Bully Boss's orders, if the Bully Boss acknowledges you at all, he or she will probably assault you verbally with phrases of criticism and condemnation, as if implying: "Are you stupid or something?"

Bully Bosses will say anything to intimidate you or to elicit signs of subservience from you. They will use the phrases mentioned above to test for your "weaknesses," and they will use them again later to have a denigrating and belittling effect on you once they have identified your "hot buttons," insecurities or abilities in which you take pride.

Bully Boss Examples

<u>The Badgerer</u>

In her darkened office and through gritted teeth, Samantha grilled Rita for the seventh time in the last four weeks:

"So, you don't think we should continue with these classes now that you've met some of the people in that group? It was *my* idea to teach those people how to set goals—they kept complaining that they weren't getting any direction from their managers, so I helped them learn to set their own direction. What would you have done?"

"I would have interviewed the employees and their managers individually to get the complete picture of what the problem was…"

"You think you know *so much*! Where do you *get* these ideas? How do you come up with them?"

"This is what I've been trained to do. I…"

"Oh, *excu-u-se me*. I only have my little college degree. What do *I* know?"

"I never said that. I never even thought that. I'm…"

After 30 minutes of this badgering, Rita said,

"I think we're saying the same things over and over again now, and I don't think we're accomplishing anything…"

"This meeting's over when I say it's over!"

…Fifteen minutes later:

"You can go now."

Before Rita got back to her office, Samantha had already sent her an e-mail message:

"I'll be out of the office most of this week, but I want to see you in my office at 3:00 on Friday afternoon to continue this conversation."

Rita thought: *Oh no, not another badgering session. That's it—I can't take it anymore. I've been a loyal manager in this company for over 20 years; I may be new to this nut case, but I don't deserve this kind of treatment!*

She replied to Samantha's e-mail message and sent a copy to Samantha's boss:

"I am afraid to meet with you one-on-one again. I don't want this conversation to turn into another badgering session. I'm asking your boss to attend this meeting to facilitate our discussion."

Neither Samantha nor her boss replied to Rita's message. Over the next two days, Rita sent two more e-mail messages to Samantha's boss and left two voice mail messages. No response. Then she went to the Human Resources Department:

"I'm afraid we can't help you. You're all white women, so there's no diversity issue—it wouldn't be appropriate for us to come between you and your managers."

At 3:05 on Friday afternoon, Samantha stormed into Rita's office and said, "Are you meeting with me now, or what?"

"Is your boss going to be there?"

"No."

"I want someone else to be there. Who would you be willing to include?"

"Are you refusing to meet with me?"

"I'm asking to have someone else present when I meet with you."

"Come into my office *now!*"

"Not unless someone else will be there to facilitate."

"This is between you and me. No one else is going to be there."

"I'm not going to subject myself to more of your abuse. I want someone to be there to keep the conversation civil."

"Then you leave me no choice. You're suspended for insubordination."

Rita fought back. She went to the legal department. One attorney offered to contact Rita's Vice President informally, although it was not within his formal authority to do so. The VP called Rita at home at 9:00 that night:

"The suspension is rescinded. You're not suspended, but take a few days off with pay. When you come back, we'll work out a transfer for you to another department."

"I can't come back to work? I can't do my job? *I'm* the one who's going to be transferred?"

"It's best to let things cool down awhile. In situations like this, we have to defend the manager. Since your manager has broader responsibilities, it would be harder to replace her than to replace one employee. We'll let you choose where you'd like to go."

Rita was sick. She didn't go back to work on Monday. She resigned soon after this incident.

The Unrealistic Ultimatum

Smitty hired Bernadine into the company to create a training department. As a newly promoted Vice President, Smitty was charged with getting the field managers up to speed. The company was growing faster than new managers could learn their jobs. Customers complained about long waits and some took their business to competitors. Managers in supporting departments complained about having to work with uninformed colleagues.

Smitty had no background in training. Bernadine had been on the job for only two months when Smitty first growled,

"When are those new job-training courses gonna to be completed?"

"I just hired people to develop these courses last week. They're professionals and they're catching on quickly, but they need time to do their jobs. We need to study those positions—identify all the tasks and determine what we need to teach."

"Look, I let you hire the people you asked for, now I need some answers. When are the courses gonna be ready?"

"We can't determine that yet. They've just begun to study those jobs. Once we know all the responsibilities that we have to teach those managers, we'll be able to estimate how long it'll take to develop the courses."

"Yeah. How much time?"

"I don't know yet."

"That's not good enough. I need to know now."

"You need to know *today*?"

"That's right."

"Why?"

"*Why*? You don't need to know "*why*" when I ask you a question. But I'll tell you anyway. I'm responsible to other people, and they're asking me—the Senior Vice President and the *President* of the company are asking me."

"What are they trying to determine? If I understood more about what they need, I might be able to give you an acceptable answer that would serve their purpose."

"You don't ask questions when the President wants an answer. You just come up with an answer."

"Would it help if I explained the process involved in developing training programs to them?"

"I'll do the explaining if there's any explaining to do."

"Well, I've been telling you what's involved."

"You're not getting the point, *Ms. Bernadine*. Do you have an answer for me or don't you?"

"If you can describe all the tasks managers must perform in each of those positions to me right now, and how to go about performing them, then I can give you an answer."

"*We'll* see about *that*!" Smitty barked as he walked away.

An hour later, Smitty flipped a memo at Bernadine from across her desk. With one end of his mouth curled up, he howled,

"This is when you're gonna have the training done by."

Bernadine read the one sentence memo:

"The job-training programs will be completed on January 15."

Smitty had signed it and addressed it to Bernadine and the Senior Vice President.

Bernadine reacted, "*Two months*? This deadline doesn't allow any time to study those positions! How do you expect us to design training programs when we don't know what to include in them?"

"That's *your* problem!" Smitty shouted over his shoulder as he stormed away.

"You're Bad"

"What's all this? Take it down—we don't know that any of this is true; I don't want people seeing this stuff" Percy bellowed.

Adele removed the charts from the meeting-room wall. Then she directed the managers to specific pages in her report. As she began to describe the problems with the programs that had been developed under his direction, Percy interrupted her:

"When I told you to find out what they didn't like about those programs, I expected you to come back with some specific recommendations…"

"I'm getting to the recommendations. I thought it would be helpful to explain the background…"

"Where are they?"

"They're summarized on page 48, but…"

"Wait. I want to *see* this…You can't draw these conclusions! This isn't supported; what kind of a study is this? I expected more from you!"

"Each of the recommendations is supported in the report. Would you like me to explain the background for each…"

Another manager, who also reported to Percy, asked,

"Adele, I see that you've recommended a standardized approach. Will each module stand alone so that each department can reference the information they need?

"Yes, that's the intent. The design allows for each program to also serve as reference…"

Percy snapped, "What page is *that* on?"

"Twenty five."

"There's nothing new about this! This is what we started out with. This is the way the programs were supposed to be designed in the first place" Percy sniped. Then he asked one of the other managers,

"Where's the original information we started out with?"

Adele offered, "I've included that information in the report. It's on page 40. I mapped each of the originally recommended modules to this design so you can compare…"

"I don't want to know about that. I want to know what happened. Why don't the existing programs follow the original design?"

The only audible sound was the ticking of the wall clock.

Percy ranted, "Okay, that's *enough* of this—I don't want to hear anymore! Give me all the copies of this report. I don't want any of you to have them" he said to the managers sitting around the conference table. "And make sure you delete your e-mail copies—I don't' want this information to get out—I don't want anyone in the other departments to know about this." Then, glaring at Adele, he said: "I want to see *you* in my office at 4:00!"

Adele thought: *"Oh no, I don't think I can take another one of his badgering sessions behind closed doors…"*

Before she could finish her thought, one of her colleagues who had attended the presentation came into her office and said,

"You did a good job—your report is excellent and your recommendations are right on—that's just what we need to do. It's sad that Percy wouldn't let you explain it, but he's the one who's responsible for the problems we're having. He underestimated the funding we would need to develop these programs. What we ended up with is all we could afford—he didn't budget any money for the technological infrastructure." Then he added, "A few of us will be here when you get out of his office—we'll wait for you no matter how long it takes. Don't let him get to you."

"Sit down" Percy commanded. Then he stared into Adele's eyes, leaned across his desk, and said in a monotone voice, "You are a bad manager. Do you hear me? You're a *bad* manager."

Percy caught a glimpse of tears welling up as Adele fought them back. He sat back in his chair, grinned, and watched her, as if he was waiting for her to cry—as if he wanted her to cry. Adele thought: *He can't evaluate me—he doesn't know what I know and he wouldn't be able to do my job. I never should have taken this job reporting to him.* She regained her composure before she spoke:

"Last week you told me my work was excellent; now you're saying it's bad?"

"You have the *potential* to be a good manager, the *potential*, but you need a lot of development."

What Bully Bosses Want from You

Bully Bosses want to control you. They want you to be powerless and to behave in their presence as if you believe you are inferior to them. They want you to acknowledge them as being superior to you in all things, not just their higher-level position in the organization or their ability to reward you. They want you to be passive and tolerant of their incivilities. They want to take from the workplace whatever they want without any interference from you— without being questioned, blocked or reported by you.

Bully Bosses want you to pledge your loyalty to them. They want you to defer to them for critical decisions about your work and follow their directions even when they are wrong. They want you to publicly support and defend their position even when better ideas are offered by others. They want you to help them put a positive spin on the accomplishments of their department even when results are unfavorable. They want you to pretend that no problems exist in their department. They want you to be able to stand-in for them and represent them exactly as they would present themselves. When their name is mentioned in their absence during a meeting or some other discussion, they want you to report to them whatever was said, word-for-word; they want you to tell who mentioned them and describe the gestures that were used by that person—including facial expressions, tone of voice, posture and body movement. They are always looking for people to tackle, and they want your help in locating those people.

Bully Bosses want you to praise them publicly in a sincere way. They want you tell others how good they are in their presence so they can hear your praise, see your demonstration of admiration and see the reactions of the others who are present. They want to be in the limelight whenever an opportunity arises for them to do so. They want to be credited with your successes and they want you to stay out of the picture when compliments are offered for your work. You will know you are doing well at accommodating the ego of Bully Bosses when you see them pretending to be shy, smiling with tight lips, slightly tilting their head and tipping it forward, raising their shoulders just a little and accepting the praise without acknowledging anyone else as a contributor.

Bully Bosses also want you to help them isolate those of your co-workers whom they have chosen as the target of their hostility. They want you to inappropriately blame their targets for problems in your department. They want you to gossip with them about their targets, spread false rumors to damage the reputation of their targets and find fault with their targets' work, character and personality attributes. They want you to lie about the quality of their targets' work when it is good, withhold information from their targets that involves your department and that may affect their targets' work, and exclude their targets from meetings and memos. By treating their targets in this way, you demonstrate your loyalty to your Bully Boss and you will remain in you boss's good favor.

Reporting to a Bully Boss

Reporting to a Bully Boss is like being one of the "Three Little Pigs" living in a house made of straw or twigs. Bully Bosses will huff and puff and blow your self-esteem down, unless they hit a wall of bricks. You may experience the same tension in the presence of a Bully Boss that you felt when you encountered a schoolyard bully in your youth. People who report to a Bully Boss experience that person in one of two ways, depending upon the type of relationship they develop with that boss: your relationship is either that of the Bully Boss's <u>buddy</u> or the Bully Boss's <u>target</u>.

If you have a "buddy" relationship with your Bully Boss, then your Bully Boss tries to convince you that you are her or his "friend" but he or she actually views you as a player-piece in a chess game. Your role is to protect the "king" (the Bully Boss)—you are expected to move in all directions around your boss to collect information and alert, defend and protect your Bully Boss. You are expected to pay careful attention to her or his likes, dislikes, moods and reactions. You must sense when you are needed to help boost your boss's ego by monitoring her or his tension level—the higher the tension level, the greater the aggressive behavior and the greater the need for ego boosting. When your Bully Boss is unhappy, you must be unhappy, too. Your top priority must be to eliminate the cause of your boss's unhappiness. Think of the kids that hung around with the bully in the schoolyard—they were the bully's buddies—you are in a similar position if you are in your Bully Boss's good favor.

There are varying degrees of Bully Boss "buddies," ranging from strong—those who actually enjoy the company of their boss, to weak—those who tolerate their Bully Boss's behavior while remaining as distant and detached as possible. The more important your job is to your department or organization, and the more interested your boss is in your work, the more likely it is that you will have a strong-buddy relationship with a Bully Boss. If your job does not get much recognition and is of little interest to your Bully Boss, then you are likely to have a weak-buddy relationship—as long as you give your Bully Boss the attention he or she wants and draw little attention to yourself. Regardless of the degree of your buddy relationship, you may fall out of favor with your Bully Boss at any time if you fail to feed her or his ego.

If you are the Bully Boss's "target," you are at the center of a dart board and the Bully Boss's piercing spears are aimed at you. Your work-life is much more miserable than that of the Bully Boss's buddies. Your boss continually badgers and berates you in antagonistic ways, while making piercing eye-contact with you and laboring over minute details of your work. He or she invents negative stories about your work and your behavior—false accusations which may include making mistakes, falsifying information, and/or behaving inappropriately or undesirably. Your boss withholds important information from you and excludes you from meetings and memos. When you question these actions, your boss's temper flares as he or she vehemently denies your charges and assaults your character and integrity. He or she may say: "Why are you the only one who seems to have this problem with me? This is *your* problem—your peers do not have any complaints."

Your Bully Boss twists your words, trying to make it seem as though you have said things that you have not spoken and never intended to say—a technique similar to brainwashing. This boss makes pointless arguments to create confusion and to make it impossible for you to reason with her or him. He or she is rude, non-responsive and inattentive when you speak. Your Bully Boss demands a higher standard of performance from you than from your co-workers, and establishes deadlines and criteria for your work that are impossible for you to meet. He or she tries to make you doubt yourself and wonder whether your perceptions are inaccurate. If you maintain your confidence during these badgering sessions, your Bully Boss will attack more forcefully and for longer durations. Make no mistake about it: you have been singled out and this mistreatment is not imagined—it is very real.

You may wonder what you did to your boss to become a target. You do your job well, and you are intelligent, more knowledgeable and experienced than your boss, and confident. You cooperate and collaborate with others and you are considerate and honest. You go about your job minding your own business, staying focused on your task and doing that which you believe is best for your organization. Surprisingly, these are the reasons why you have been targeted for aggression by your boss! Because of your integrity and ability, it is difficult for your Bully Boss to feel superior to you, and it is equally difficult for her or him to make you feel inferior, so your Bully Boss strikes out in an attempt to beat you down and diminish your capacity. You did not realize that your Bully Boss experiences the workplace as a game board, or as a series of contests that he or she wants to win, nor did you know that your boss expected you to help her or him "win" personal triumphs at work. You may think that it is inconceivable that a boss would behave in this way, so you did not look for the signs. That is the reason you are in this situation and have become your boss's target. Your boss took advantage of your optimism and naiveté to tear you down while you were unaware that he or she was doing so. The harder you worked to accomplish your goals, assist your coworkers, and impress your boss with your ability and confidence, the more it appeared to your Bully

Boss that you were "winning" and he or she was "losing" the favorable attention that you attracted—and this made your Bully Boss furious. Your Bully Boss took advantage of your good nature and belittled your abilities and accomplishments because that was the only way he or she knew how to feel superior to you. Few people, if any, are able to survive this kind of treatment for very long, and Bully Bosses know this.

The Bully Boss Survival Quiz

Examine your relationship with your Bully Boss objectively in this "True-or-False" quiz:

Statement:	T	F
1. You work productively and comfortably with a boss who misdirects people, demands your subservience and is rude.		
2. You do not mind being insulted, taunted, or harassed by your boss.		
3. You do not mind your boss snapping, shouting or cursing at you.		
4. It is okay with you that your boss belittles you without cause or criticizes your work even when the quality is excellent.		
5. You believe that employees must accept rude and insulting behavior from their manager.		
6. You are willing to help your boss single out one person in your department as her or his target for aggression.		
7. You are willing to overlook your boss's nastiness as long as you are benefiting by it in some way.		
8. You know that your boss will be gone in less than a year and you are certain that you can tolerate her or him for that long.		

If you responded "True" to most of these statements, there is a good chance that you might survive reporting to a Bully Boss in the short term without too much harm being done to you. But don't be misled—you will suffer the consequences of negative stress if you work with this boss for a long period of time (depending on your tolerance level and general health and well-being, a long period of time could be one to two years). Those consequences may include health issues that may seem unrelated to your work.

If you responded "False" to **any** of these statements, it is very likely that you will be negatively impacted in your current position in the near future.

Strategies for Surviving Your Bully Boss

You can survive a Bully Boss by staying on her or his friendly side, but that will last only as long as you remain subservient. Consider these factors:

- You can survive better if you become a "buddy" to your Bully Boss by pledging your loyalty and support, publicly defending your Bully Boss, and admiring her or his incivility (or at least pretending).

- A buddy relationship with a Bully Boss is very volatile; you must pander to your boss's needs and wants to keep from falling out of favor.

- You must act immediately, at the first incident of disrespect, to stop a Bully Boss from making you the target of her or his hostility.

- Once you become a Bully Boss's target, you cannot reverse the situation; escalations and interventions will not work— your only options are to leave or tolerate abuse.

- You do not cause your Bully Boss to target you—your competence and confidence are the triggers; your Bully Boss does not want you to appear more capable than he or she is.

When you recognize that you are becoming a Bully Boss's target, you can take steps to switch roles and become a buddy, but you must do so immediately. Bully Bosses will allow you to completely change your relationship with them early in your relationship. They will not comment about the change in your behavior as long as you let them think that you believe they are superior to you in all ways. If you can credit your Bully Boss with your successes, seek her or his advice in the conduct of your work, and give your Bully Boss undeserved public praise, then he or she will accept that you have "changed your evil ways" and become a valued employee. You must decide whether you can be true to yourself while attending to your Bully Boss's ego.

If you think that changing your behavior in this way would be too belittling or too high a price to pay, then your situation will only get worse. A Bully Boss wants you to breakdown, be less than you are, and to succumb to her or his control. Consider leaving the organization and prepare to avoid becoming a target in your next job.

How to Avoid Becoming a Target

You must immediately address any act of hostility, harassment or coercion that is directed toward you by a Bully Boss—on the first incident of its occurrence. If you tolerate an incident and prolong your response, you will be targeted for future attacks. Tell your boss that you will not tolerate her or his behavior. Be straight forward and direct. These aggressors are likely to leave you alone and move on to an easier target when they understand that you will not tolerate their behavior—they seek out and prey on people who appear to be weak, and they interpret tolerance as weakness. Your verbal confrontation may be enough to end the situation if you do it immediately; however, if you let the aggression continue for a while before standing up for yourself, you will find that a verbal warning is ineffective later.

If there is a second incident after your verbal warning, then write a memo to your Bully Boss in which you describe your understanding of what was said and/or done, and describe the behavior that you found to be offensive or unacceptable. In the memo, state the day, date, time, and location of the incident. Allow for the possibility that you may have misunderstood, but only for this first written memo. Bullies are very much afraid of anything in written form that accuses or incriminates them. Written charges are powerful and they are a useful tool for non-aggressive people to use. Writing gives you a chance to calm down after the incident and state your concerns clearly and rationally. Following is an example:

Memo

Date: January 12, 2005

From: Good Employee (Your name)

To: Bad Boss (Your boss's name)

Subject: Unacceptable Behavior

This memo is to inform you of the effect you had on me yesterday and to begin a dialogue to establish guidelines for future interactions between us.

When we talked in your office at 3:10 PM on Wednesday, January 14, I was shocked and disappointed when you shouted, *"What kind of an idiot are you?!"* That outburst was not only undeserved, but it was unacceptable to me and unprofessional of you. I may have misunderstood you or overreacted, but this is the second time I have brought this behavior to your attention. I would like for you to understand my concern, and I am requesting that our future interactions be strictly professional.

If there is a third incident, then write a memo similar to the previous one, but this time send a copy of the memo to your boss's manager and/or to a Human Resource Department manager who deals with conflict in your organization. State in the memo that this is the third incident of unacceptable behavior, and attach a copy of your first memo. A Bully Boss is likely to be willing to smooth this situation over and come to terms with you when he or she realizes that you are serious and will not be mistreated without imposing consequences on her or him. This may be all you need to do when tested by a Bully Boss to avoid becoming a permanent target.

If there is a fourth incident, then you may not be able to avoid becoming a target of this Bully Boss. The best you can do at this stage is to request a face-to-face meeting with your boss and to have that meeting facilitated by an objective third party, but not by your boss's manager—have it facilitated by someone you trust in the Human Resource Department, or someone from outside the organization who specializes in conflict resolution and who will work with you on a contractual basis. Request that the organization pay for an outside specialist; however, it would be appropriate to pay for this service yourself if this is your only remaining option. Be sure that you know in advance who the facilitator of this meeting will be if you cannot choose this person, and be sure that this person is someone you believe will be fair. Before the meeting, make a list of the things that are being said or done to you which you find unacceptable. Verbally present these actions in the meeting and demand that they stop—this is an appropriate time for you to make demands—be confident and firm. After the meeting, write and distribute minutes to everyone who was involved in the meeting and highlight any agreements that were made. Write these minutes even if someone else claims that it is her or his role to document the minutes—their version of what happened may exclude points that are important to you. It will be best if your version is issued first so that you will not appear to be challenging the minutes. This course of action may get you transferred to another department even though you will not have your boss's recommendation.

When you choose to document your boss's abusive behavior, be prepared for a higher-level manager in your organization to advise you to stop doing so. This manager will most likely perceive that you are preparing for litigation against the organization and will be more inclined to protect and defend the organization than to support you. If you are advised to stop documenting your boss's incidents of hostility, then tell this manager that you want to put these incidents out of your thoughts so that you may focus on your work, and that writing them down enables you to do so. Emphasize that your intent is to prevent the situation from interfering with the conduct of business, and that you are following good business practices in documenting these issues, just as you would be if you were documenting any other business problem.

If this approach does not end the hostility, harassment or coercion, then consider seeking outside assistance from another organization. The Equal Employment Opportunity Commission (EEOC) oversees hostile workplace issues, the American Civil Liberties Union (ACLU) defends employees when their rights are being violated, and an attorney may be able to influence your management to take corrective action. Before you go to an attorney, determine whether you have signed an employment agreement when you were hired that prohibits litigation against the organization and requires that arbitration be used to resolve disputes. If that is the case, then arrange to interview the arbitrator before the proceedings begin to determine whether he or she is someone you can trust. Ask for examples of similar situations that the arbitrator has resolved, and ask the arbitrator to explain what will happen in your case.

Keep a copy of all relevant memos and meeting minutes at your home or in another safe place away from your work location. If your documentation is stored electronically, then also store it on paper. Present this documentation and any written responses that you may have received to the person you choose to represent you. Remain focused on the fact that your intention is to stop the undesirable behavior and eliminate its interference with the organization's objectives. It is more effective to confront this behavior in the context of emphasizing its cost to the organization than to present it as a personal or personality issue which is likely to be perceived as too insignificant for a formal intervention. Emphasize that time spent on intentional acts of hostility, harassment, and coercion is time taken away from the organization and that it interferes with the fulfillment of the organization's purpose and goals. In other words, demonstrate that you boss's behavior is bad for the organization—not just bad for you.

At the same time that you are trying to stop the unacceptable behavior, privately update your resume and begin scanning other departments and/or the external job market for other positions. Leaving the organization may be your best option if you cannot obtain support or stop the behavior.

In Case of Physical Assault

While it is unlikely to occur, your Bully Boss may become violent. Violence in unacceptable! Period! No one has the right to physically hurt you in the workplace. If your boss assaults you physically, call the police immediately and report the incident. File civil charges against your boss if he or she has hurt you badly but, before you make that call, understand that management will not be happy about your decision to involve the police. However, management is not equipped to handle this type of situation, and physical violence is a personal matter that just happens to occur in the workplace. After you contact the police, get medical attention even if you are not certain whether you were badly hurt—you may be in shock and unable to detect the extent to which you have been harmed. If you are bruised, cut, or broken, then have pictures taken and mark them with the date and time of the incident. Make sure that records of the incident are on file with authorities outside of your organization. This will send a clear message to your attacker that you will not become her or his victim.

If you are afraid to be in the presence of your boss after the attack, take *copies* of the police report, medical report, and/or pictures to a Human Resource Department manager and request that some action be taken to ensure that you and your boss will not be alone together on company premises at any time. You may be transferred to another job or placed on a temporary leave-of-absence as a result of this action. Accept this outcome as a lesser evil than being subjected to the potential for a repeated assault. Seek legal assistance if you believe that you are being penalized for your boss's behavior or if no action is taken to protect you from your violent boss.

Strategies that Won't Work

Do not "turn the other cheek" when a Bully affronts you. Passivity and tolerance of disrespectful or abusive behavior are invitations to a Bully Boss to do it again. Do not launch a counter attack, either. Be assertive, but not aggressive—in other words, stand your ground and state that the way your boss behaves toward you is unacceptable and unprofessional, but do not insult or offend your boss in the same way he or she has treated you. Your Bully Boss is an expert at intimidation, so to the Bully Boss an insult or offensive attack initiates a game that your boss is certain he or she can win.

Escalating your concerns will probably be more damaging for you than for your Bully Boss. Bully Bosses are usually admired by the managers they report to because of their apparent ability to "get results" and because they are subservient and deferential to their bosses. Bully Bosses also have "buddies" among your co-workers who will defend them against any charges you make against them. For these reasons, it is unlikely that management will believe you.

A Bully Boss does not want you in the organization, so it is very likely that he or she will sabotage any attempt you make to transfer to another department. Bully Bosses will not letup on you until you become their buddy or resign.

Interview Strategies

What to listen for:

- Someone trying extra hard to impress you with her or his accomplishments.

- An extremely stressful interview due to intense questioning for a long period of time with no break.
- Hypothetical situations used in questioning with constant what-ifs thrown in after every response you give.
- Someone who seems to playing a game with you to see how much you know, rather than being direct.

Bully Bosses can be difficult to detect during interviews because they are trying to make a good impression on you much of the time. If the manager seems to be stressing her or his competence as greater than yours will ever be, even if you have specialized skills and knowledge, beware.

Accepting the Consequences of Staying

Bully Bosses may be found in any workplace and at any level. No workplace is exempt from employing Bully Bosses, regardless of the industry, profession, or field, and no one is exempt from being targeted by a Bully Boss. The effects of unprovoked and undeserved hostility from a boss can be emotionally, physiologically, and economically devastating to anyone. Individuals who are targeted are not the cause of a Bully Boss's hostility. Bully Bosses pick on people regardless of their age, experience or credentials. The more experienced and accomplished people are, the more likely it is that they will be perceived as threats to a Bully Boss's desire to be superior. It is, therefore, more likely that highly competent people will become targets, and that their work and reputation will be undermined by a Bully Boss. Bully Bosses typically seek as targets people who are more inclined to be cooperative than combative, who offer little or no resistance to the Bully Boss's attacks, who are of high integrity, and who are nonpolitical. Bullying behavior has been widely studied and is well documented; you can learn a lot about it from books and Web sites.

If you are one of your Bully Boss's "buddies," then recognize that you are in a volatile relationship with a person who could turn against you at any time. Create a network of contacts in your organization, especially in departments you might be qualified to transfer into. Make others aware of your contributions even if you boss has taken credit for your work.

If, or when, you become your Bully Boss's target, then you must recognize that you are in an abusive relationship. There is no good reason for anyone to remain in an abusive relationship indefinitely. If you have tolerated three or more incidents of your boss's abusive behavior, then it is unlikely that you will be able to change the nature of that relationship. If you choose to continue to report to your Bully Boss, then you must accept that you are choosing to be treated with disrespect. It is not your fault that your boss treats you as badly as he or she does, but it is your fault that you accept this behavior. Consider counseling as a way of gaining insight into your reasons for tolerating this behavior and as a developmental tool for learning to handle similar situations more effectively.

9: THE MANIPULATOR

"I'm indispensable!"

How to Recognize a Manipulator Boss

Garrett went around the accepted procedures when he hired Terra last week, and now needed to get all the paperwork submitted to the Human Resource Department:

"I just need you to sign your job description, Terra, to finalize the paperwork and make you an official employee!"

"Well that's certainly important! Where do I sign?"

"Right here" he said, pointing to the line on the bottom of page three.

"I'd just like to take a look at it first. Can you give me a minute?"

"Sure."

"Garrett?

"Yes?"

"This isn't the position you hired me for; this job description is for an Assistant; you hired me as the Director."

"Oh, don't pay any attention to that. This is just a formality. It doesn't mean anything. You just need to sign so I can get you added to the payroll."

"But these duties aren't anything like the job description I have back in my office. I'm really concerned about signing this."

"Don't worry. You'll still perform all the duties of the Director…

"But…"

"Trust me; it doesn't mean anything—it's just a piece of paper. I take care of my people; it'll be fine."

Manipulator Bosses do whatever they can to make their job easy and to appear indispensable. They fabricate information or do not tell the whole story—they tell some of the truth, but not the whole truth. They leave out important information to make you rely on them to complete projects and they give you incorrect information when the facts will work against their desire to appear indispensable. They try to convince you that their ideas are your own in an attempt to get what they want. They seem driven more by the need to be needed than the desire to make a meaningful contribution.

Manipulator Bosses ask their employees to meet unreasonable deadlines so they can impress their managers with their ability to get quick results. When they get caught doing or saying something that is wrong, they don't admit it—they wait until the heat blows over and then continue doing whatever they were doing before. They avoid direct conflict and masterfully practice passive aggression.

Manipulator Bosses talk about the department they manage as if it is their own enterprise and not part of the larger organization. Everything is personal to them—work is an extension of their identity, employees are invaders of their personal domain, and questions are threats of war. Manipulator Bosses maintain as much distance as possible from their manager to preserve their sovereign reign, while hoarding information to make the people who report to them dependent on them. Their department is their kingdom, and the people who report to them are their serfs.

Manipulator Bosses maintain a low-key, Pollyanna-like demeanor. Their managers' tend to regard female Manipulator Bosses as "sweet" and male Manipulator Bosses as "gentle." Manipulators tend to speak in sing-song rhythm when greeting people, engaging in small talk and making light of heavy issues:

"Oh, HI! Isn't TODAY a LOVELY day?!"

"So SORRY about NO raise…GUESS we SHOULD be GLAD we STILL have JOBS!"

These bosses evade discussions about controversial subjects, and rarely, if ever, raise their voices. They change the subject in the middle of conversations when responding to questions they don't like and then they go on as if you had been talking about their newly-introduced subject all along, for example:

Question: "Did you know that customer called to complain?"

Manipulator Boss's response: "Did you see this month's results? We should be really proud of the work we're doing here! Why don't we have lunch at that new place today?"

Manipulator Bosses avoid open conflict and are masterful double-talkers. They try to put words in your mouth to get you to agree with them, take the blame for something that is not your fault, or evade a topic they don't want to deal with, for example:

Employee: "I need you to help me deal with the group's hostility toward me."

Manipulator Boss: "It must be difficult working with people who are younger than you; you don't like that they have less experience…"

Manipulator Bosses use silence as both a defensive and an offensive weapon. When you question their actions, they stare at you without speaking, blinking, breathing, or twitching a muscle. In their stillness and gaze, they are like mountain lions that have cornered their prey and are steadying for the kill. They grin when they see that you are uncomfortable. When asked for advice or given a chance to assist someone they don't like, they either remain silent or withhold important information, but they indirectly let you know they're being evasive by behaving in an uncharacteristically coy way and pasting a flat smile below an icy stare.

Manipulator Bosses won't defend the employees who report to them under any circumstances, yet they expect their employees to agree with their ideas at all times and about all things. Their loyalty is only to themselves.

Manipulator Bosses disguise the direct orders they give by phrasing them as questions. They say negative things in positive ways to conceal their opinions and exploitations. Listen for phrases like these:

- "I'm sure you agree…"
- "You *do* think this is the right thing to do…"
- "I'm sure you wouldn't have it any other way…"
- "You want what's best, don't you?"
- "Take my word for it…"
- "There may be a better way, but this way works…"
- "This is just a formality; don't take it too seriously…"
- "I didn't mean it *literally*."

These are the Manipulator Boss's verbal weapons.

MANIPULATOR EXAMPLES

Filling the Vacancy

"Hello Vera. This is Myra Schultz calling. We met a few months ago at a networking meeting. Do you remember me?"

"Yes, I do! How are you?"

"I'm fine, thanks. I may have an opportunity for you. Are you still looking for another job?

"Yes, I am."

"My Director of Events is leaving next week and I need someone who can replace her right away. I think you'd be good in this job. Are you interested?"

"Yes, I'm definitely interested, but I'd like a little more information. Can we meet some time this week?"

"I was hoping you'd say that! Can you be here tomorrow at 10:00 to meet with the outgoing Director and me?"

"I sure can."

Vera accepted the job and agreed to start the following Monday. At the end of her first week on the job, Myra told Vera that she now reported to another manager, Kate, whom she would meet next week. When Vera met with her new boss, Kate said,

"So, I understand that you have a Master's degree. There's probably not much that *I* can teach *you*; I only went to high school. Do you have any questions?"

"Yes. How did it come about that I'm working in Myra's department but reporting to you?"

"We thought it would be a good idea for you to work with someone who's familiar with our procedures. You have the same job I do, but in a different department."

"Since we have the same job, yet I report to you, I'm not sure how we should work together. How would you like to handle this?"

"Well, to be honest with you, I'm not happy with this situation. Myra should have consulted with me before she hired you. I don't think you're the right person for this job, but nobody asked *me*."

Things went downhill quickly after that. Kate was sarcastic with Vera every time they spoke and routinely misinformed her, causing Vera to have to rework her plans continually. Three weeks later, Vera met with Myra and said,

"I accepted this position with the understanding that I would report to you. I wouldn't have taken the job if I'd met Kate first. She doesn't like the idea that you hired me without her approval, and it seems like she's trying to make me fail just to prove that you were wrong. If I have to continue to report to her, I'm going to resign."

Myra responded, "Let me look into it. I'll see what I can do."

A few days later, Myra called Vera into her office and said,

"It's taken care of. You don't report to Kate anymore; you report to me."

Vera replied, "What a relief! Thank you!"

Vera stopped meeting with Kate and stopped sending reports to her. She gave her reports to Myra, instead.

Two weeks later, Myra told Vera that Kate wanted to meet with them. Kate invited the Human Resource Director and the Division Vice President to the same meeting. Kate began the meeting saying,

"I've invited you all here to discuss a disciplinary problem." Then she read a report she had prepared. In it, she accused Vera of being uncooperative and insubordinate. She finalized her report saying, "We can't go on working this way. Something's got to change."

Vera said, "I don't understand what this is all about. I don't report to you; I report to Myra."

Kate replied, "That's news to me! When did that happen?"

Vera looked at Myra, and Myra looked down at the floor. Kate, the HR Director, and the VP looked back and forth at each other, and then the HR Director and VP said at the same time,

"But that change never happened."

Vera had reported to Kate all along.

Myra manipulated Vera to keep her from resigning and leaving a vacant position in her department.

The Literal Misunderstanding

Just before Vaughn left the office, he sent an e-mail message to his staff saying:

"I'll be back on Friday. You won't be able to reach me while I'm away. The day I get back, I'm scheduled to present the status of the new curriculum to our Vice President. I expect to see a draft of the courses you're working on as soon as I get back."

When Wesley got the message, he tried to reach Vaughn by phone before he left. Unable to reach him, he sent an e-mail message hoping that Vaughn would check it before he left. In the message, Wesley said:

"You just assigned this course to me, and I haven't even begun the design. It will be impossible for me to have a draft available on Friday. Please let me know what else you can use for your presentation on Friday, and I'll get it ready for you."

When Wesley did not receive a response from Vaughn by the following morning, he realized that he would have to prepare at least a tentative draft by Friday. He sent a message to his colleagues saying he would be unavailable to meet with them during the next few days while he worked on this deadline, and he sent a copy of the message to Vaughn.

Wesley spent every minute of the next four days feverishly drafting a course for which he had no outline, working well into the evening hours. He sent another e-mail message to Vaughn on Thursday evening so he would have it first thing Friday morning. He explained that he had developed a skeleton draft for the presentation, but that it was tentative and would probably change. Vaughn sent a reply before starting hours on Friday saying:

"I don't have to make that presentation today after all, but I appreciate that we now have a draft available for that course. Please see me as soon as you get this message."

Wesley went to Vaughn's office immediately after reading the message. Vaughn said,

"I thought it was inappropriate for you to tell you colleagues that you would not be available to meet with them while I was away. That was an extreme and unnecessary measure."

"But you needed a draft and there was no way I could get it done without eliminating all distractions."

"No, I never asked you for a draft. A status report would have been good enough."

"I'm sure your message said *draft*. Let me check it again."

Wesley sent a copy of Vaughn's original message back to him and underlined the word: <u>draft</u>.

Vaughn replied, "I'm glad that I can report your rapid progress on this project, but I didn't expect you take my words *literally!*"

Wesley later learned that Vaughn was never scheduled to make a presentation on Friday.

The Pseudo-Participatory Manager

Stella, a Vice President, interviewed Marjorie for an assignment. She explained,

"I need someone to facilitate a meeting for me so that I can participate just like the others. I want everyone to feel equal in sharing their ideas; I don't want them to think that whatever I say is the way it should be because I'm the boss and then withhold their suggestions. I want to make a lot of changes in this department in job assignments and the way we work with our customers."

Marjorie asked, "Do you already know what the changes are that you're going to make?"

"Yes"

"If the people who report to you suggest other ideas during this meeting, will you consider their ideas as possible options for your plan?"

"No."

"Then what's the point of having this meeting and asking these people to share their ideas?"

"I want them to think that the plan is their idea."

"Let me see if I understand your request: You want me to facilitate a meeting under the pretense that it is for the purpose of allowing the managers who report to you to contribute their ideas, but you don't really want their ideas; you just want to tell them what your plan is in a way that will make them think that it is actually their idea. Is that right?"

"Yes! Exactly! That's why I thought I'd use an outside person!"

"Would you mind telling me what your plan is?"

"No, not at all…"

When Stella finished describing her plan, Marjorie suggested alternative approaches to use with the group rather than tricking them into thinking Stella's plan was their idea. Stella didn't like any of Marjorie's suggestions. When Marjorie asked why, Stella said,

"I don't want to spend time dealing with these people issues! I know they've got their own ideas about what we should do, but I know what needs to be done here and it's going to happen whether they like it or not! I just want them to think they had input into so they'll have a sense of ownership in carrying out the plan and won't fight me."

What Manipulator Bosses Want from You

Manipulator Bosses want you to be dependent on them while accomplishing things they want done. They want you believe that you cannot be successful in your job without their guidance and oversight, regardless of your position or level of competence. They give you incomplete information to make you keep coming back to them for help or incorrect information that misleads you.

They want you to help them convince their managers that their department could not function without them. When you are not helping to reinforce their necessity, they want you to be invisible; undetectable; imperceptible. They have no genuine interest in you—

you are just a necessary evil to get a job done, a job they would rather do themselves but are stuck with the responsibility of overseeing because one person can't do it all.

Manipulator Bosses want you to smile at them and nod your head in agreement whenever they speak. They want you to do whatever they ask you to do without questioning them. They want you to praise them for their wisdom and emulate them. They want you to act just like them: pretend everything is wonderful, never confront anyone in their presence and tiptoe happily through wilted tulips when things in the workplace aren't as they should be. They want you to say "Yes, Ma'am" or "Yes, Sir" with a sincere quality in your voice when they ask you to do things. They want you to put a positive spin on everything that happens as if seeing events through rose-colored glasses.

Manipulator Bosses want you to be indebted to them. They want you to acknowledge that you could not do your job without their guidance. They want you to indirectly credit them with your accomplishments by acknowledging all they have taught you—whether or not they have done so.

Reporting to a Manipulator Boss

Reporting to a Manipulator Boss is like being "Little Red Riding Hood;" you think you're visiting with sweet, little-ole Grandma, but something isn't quite right. When you try to put your finger on it, this "wolf-in-sheep's clothing" makes bad things sound good, just like in the fairly tale:

Red Riding Hood: "What big eyes you have!"

Wolf: "The better to see you with, my dear."

Manipulator Bosses try to make your strengths sound like weaknesses to convince you that you need their guidance. They want you to be needy so they can reinforce the myth that they are indispensable. For example, if you are methodical and good with details, they might say: "Stop being so nit-picky! If you are good at identifying or preventing problems, they might ask: "Why are you always looking for trouble?" or "Can't you leave well-enough alone?"

When giving you an assignment or explaining how to do something, Manipulator Bosses give you either incomplete or incorrect information. If the information is incomplete, you will have to keep coming back to them for more details; if it is incorrect, you will need them to help you correct what you have done. Either way, they create a situation in which you are dependent on them to do your job.

When you do something well, their praise is followed by a question indicating that you could have done better, or they credit themselves with having helped you accomplish the task. For example, they might say: "That report looks good but there are no graphs. Did you consider including graphs in the package?" or "Good report. It looks like the extra time I spent with you really paid off, didn't it?" Your work is never good enough to satisfy a Manipulator Boss.

The Manipulator Boss Survival Quiz

Examine your relationship with your Manipulator Boss objectively in this "True-or-False" quiz:

Statement:	T	F
1. You are willing to be quiet when you disagree with your boss.		
2. You are willing to be quiet when your boss says something wrong, misleads others or causes harm to your organization.		
3. You will defend your boss when he or she misinforms others.		
4. As long as you can truthfully say you were just following orders, you'll do whatever your boss tells you to do, even if it's wrong.		
5. You are willing to take risks, try new approaches, and/or suggest new ideas knowing that your boss will not defend you if you fail.		
6. You will not question your boss when he or she tells you things that seem incorrect.		
7. You will sign documents your boss asks you to sign without reading them, or when you disagree with what they say.		
8. It is okay with you that your boss sometimes doesn't answer your questions.		

If you responded "True" to most of these statements, then there is a good chance that you might survive reporting to a Manipulator Boss without too much negative stress.

If you responded "False" to **any** of these statements, then it is very likely that you will be negatively impacted in your current position in the near future.

Strategies for Surviving Your Manipulator Boss

If you responded "False" to any of the statements in the Survival Quiz, then you will not be able to report to a Manipulator Boss for a very long time without experiencing some negative side effects. If you believe that your boss is "just passing though" your department and will move on to another job soon, here are some things you can do to avoid harm in the short term:

- Be quiet when you disagree with your boss or when he or she says something to others that is wrong, or misleading.

- Find a way to be able to backup something your boss says when he or she misinforms others.

- To prevent any harm that your boss may cause, speak to others confidentially about making changes without your boss's knowledge.

- Do not question your Manipulator Boss's instructions— ever—even if they don't make any sense. Do what you must to get the job done and make it seem as though your boss helped you.

- Do not ask your boss to support any new ideas or suggestions you make.

- Do not expect your boss to answer questions; find other sources if you need answers.

- Verify everything your boss tells you, but don't get caught doing it, and don't reveal to anyone in your organization that your boss misinformed you while you are verifying the information.

- Read carefully anything your boss asks you to sign before you sign it. Stall if he or she asks you to sign something you do not want to sign to buy time to think of a way out of the situation or let it expire.

If your boss plans to keep this job for a long time, consider transferring to another department. When requesting a transfer, tell your boss that you are interested in continuing to learn about the organization. Do *not* say that you think you have learned all you can in your current job—your boss believes that you can never know as much as he or she does. Tell your boss you hope he or she will continue to offer guidance and support to you in your new position—you don't have to follow-through with this request; asking is just an ego booster acknowledging her or his sense of self-importance to win your boss's support in helping you transfer.

Strategies That Won't Work

Escalation won't work. Your Manipulator Boss has probably convinced her or his manager that he or she is indispensable. That means that the people who report to your boss are incapable of doing their jobs without your boss's guidance as far as her or his boss is concerned. Your boss's manager will not take your charges seriously and will wonder why you don't appreciate the support your boss provides. You cannot change this perception—the lack of problems reported about your boss's department convinces her or his manager that he or she is doing the right thing.

Interview Strategies

What to listen for:

Since they are masters of vagueness, Manipulator Bosses can be difficult to identify during interviews, but it can be done. Ask the following questions and pay attention to the responses:

- How do you prefer to deal with the situation when the people who report to you don't agree with your decisions?
- How much opportunity will I have to make my own decisions in this job?
- How do you demonstrate that you trust the people who report to you?
- How have you supported someone who reported to you when they were challenged by someone outside the department or unintentionally caused a problem?
- How do you pass along information that the people who report to you need to do their jobs?

Use open-ended-questions—questions that require a statement in response rather than a single word like yes or no—when interviewing with a manager whom you suspect might be a Manipulator Boss. Ask for specific, detailed information and examples—if you don't get the specifics, beware.

Accepting the Consequences of Staying

If you choose to stay with a Manipulator Boss, you must be willing to act "invisible" when your work is good, and take the blame for problems created by your boss. Accept that your boss will intentionally mislead you, and that you will be told to do things incorrectly. Get comfortable with the idea that you will be allowed to know only some of the facts about the projects you work on but never the "big picture."

If you *must* continue to report to a Manipulator Boss, consider counseling as an outlet for your frustration—a relationship with a Manipulator Boss is psychologically abusive. But be aware that a counselor is likely to encourage you to plan to get away from this boss sooner rather than later. You cannot change another person; you can only change yourself. If you enjoy your work, then the need to move on can be difficult to accept. Unless you can find a similar job elsewhere, you may eventually have to give up work you enjoy to maintain your self-respect.

If you compromise your values or standards to continue to work with a Manipulator Boss, then you must accept responsibility for the fallout of your decision: diminishing self-esteem; and the side-effects of destructive, compensating activities such as substance abuse, including failing health and deteriorating relationships in your personal life.

10: THE CULT MAKER

"Let's find someone to blame all our problems on!"

How to Recognize a Cult-Maker Boss

"I'm here because Nelly just left my office so upset she was almost in tears. She's says you're accusing her of doing something she didn't do. What's going on, Celia?"

"I can't imagine why, Emily, I haven't accused Nelly of anything. I'm just trying to find out what happened with one of my projects. I saw that Nelly posted it on the schedule with Jerry's name listed as the developer and contact person, so I sent her an e-mail message and asked her if this was a mistake."

"This isn't the first time you've upset Nelly, and your peers are uncomfortable around you, too."

"What exactly did I do to make anyone upset or uncomfortable?"

"It's your attitude, the way you say things."

"Here's a copy of my message, Emily:

>*Nelly,*
>*I see that one of my projects is scheduled and it*
>*has Jerry's name on it. Is this a mistake? Did*
>*you mean to schedule a different project?*

"Do you see anything in this message that's offensive?"

"It's your tone."

"What tone? All I did was state a fact and ask a question!"

"That's exactly it—facts. Don't state facts. Facts are offensive, especially when they're in writing. Make everything sound like a question and you'll get along a lot better with your co-workers and with me. Try to be a team player."

Cult-Maker Bosses create a following of marginally capable or unqualified, but loyal, employees to shelter them while they do as they please at the expense of the organization that employs them. They create a superficial sense of esprit de corps among their employees, emphasizing the word "team" to describe their

161

department. But rather than developing collaborative teams, Cult-Maker Bosses surround themselves with "groupies"—obedient followers who feel indebted to them for their job. Groupies are stronger than cliques. Groupies function like gang members who help their chosen leader fortify her or his turf by wielding weapons of psychological devastation against challengers. Cult-Makers defend their groupies even when they are wrong in exchange for groupies doing the same for them.

Cult-Maker Bosses convince their managers that they are experts at the leading edge of their field who can guide their organization into the creation of new innovations, but they are actually unqualified for the position they hold. To hide their limitations, they create a "turfdom" within their organization and become its dictator. They shelter themselves from outside interference so they cannot be "found out." They create barriers to infiltration by imposing a top-secret-like, proprietary exclusivity on their department that shelters it from interference.

Cult-Maker Bosses encourage infighting between their loyal gang of followers and competent employees who may question or challenge them. They set these competent employees up as scapegoats for the group's poor performance and ostracize these employees for refusing to conspire with them. They get their "gang" of followers to create a hostile work environment to force out employees who won't collude with them.

You will often hear Cult-Maker Bosses say things such as:

- "We're not doing things in conventional ways here; we're at the leading edge of a new approach."

- "Of course you don't understand; this is new."

- "We'll be successful if we do things my way."

- "Why is it that you're the only one who has this problem?"

- "I've heard reports about you and I want you to stop…"

- "You need to be more cooperative."

- "You don't fit in."

- "Your work is good, but your attitude stinks."

- "You're only as good as your reputation, and I can change that."

- "You're not a team player."

Cult-Maker Bosses use these verbal weapons to intimidate you and send the message that you are not wanted because they see you as a threat to exposing their charade. Observe carefully any manager who says these things, but be especially alert to managers who use the expression "team player." Some managers are casual when they use this phrase, but when Cult-Maker Bosses say "team player" they slow down their pace, lower their voice, and glare at you—as if implying a threat. The term "team player" does not mean "teamwork" when it is used by a Cult-Maker Boss; it indicates that collusion is "in play" and that you are expected to comply with dysfunctional norms to help secure your Cult-Maker Boss's "turfdom." In a business context, "teamwork" refers to collaborative and cooperative effort directed toward achieving an organization's purpose and goals both effectively and efficiently. But Cult-Maker Bosses could not survive if their employees practiced authentic teamwork and focused on the organization's goals rather than their personal goals—their turfdom would disintegrate without collusive "team players." They wouldn't be able to use their position for personal power and undeserved privileges.

Cult-Maker Bosses speak charismatically, but their depth of knowledge is shallow—they cannot substantiate what they say. They declare themselves as experts who have an innovative approach. They fool their unknowing managers into accepting them as innovators by telling them that other experts in their field are outdated, stuck in the past or unable to understand the Cult-Maker's new ways.

Cult-Maker Boss Examples

Get With the Program

Greta was ten minutes early for a monthly status meeting; she was the last one to enter the conference room. She sat in the only seat available—the seat farthest from the door, on the side of the long conference table, to the left of the Project Manager who sat at the end. It seemed odd to her that the other project-team members were sitting there so quietly. There was none of the usual mingling; everyone sat at the table attentively, as if in anticipation of a profound event. It was too quiet. All eyes were on her as she sat down. She looked back at the 18 men gathered around the perimeter of the long, narrow table and said, "Good morning" but no one responded.

Then Harold, the Project Manager, said, "I think we can get started now. As you all know, this is our first meeting since the plan was announced for splitting the company. We have to be careful not to violate any antitrust issues with the information we share here today. We have a few new people, so let's go around the table and have each person introduce themselves; say your name, your company, and your role. We'll start on my right side with Verne and go counter-clockwise around the table."

"Hello, I'm Verne Basil. I'm with Greenleaf Corporation…"

The next person introduced himself saying, "…I'm with Greenleaf Corporation…"

And the next person said, "…I'm with Greenleaf Corporation…"

By the eighth introduction, Greta began to wonder what was going on. Her coworkers introduced themselves as members of the company that had not been created yet: Greenleaf Corporation. She knew that some people were going to be reassigned and that she might be one of them, but those decisions had not been made yet. She watched and listened as all the remaining members of the project team introduced themselves as employees of Greenleaf Corporation. Now it was her turn:

"I'm Greta Geiger and I'm with Grundering Corporation. I write the implementation plans."

During the long silence that followed no one appeared to be breathing. Then Harold asked, "Does anyone have anything to report that might change the direction of this project?"

One member asked, "Is it okay to distribute my written report to everyone who's attending this meeting?"

Harold responded, "Just give it to me. I'll keep track of who's staying and who's going to the new company and I'll see that it gets to the right people." Then he said, "Anything else?"

Heads nodded from side to side, and Harold said, "Okay, then. It looks like we're still on track and the announcement hasn't effected us at all. Let's meet again in two weeks..." Harold then announced the date, time, and location of the next meeting, and the attendees hurried out of the conference room.

Greta was the last one to leave. Harold followed her out of the conference room and stopped her in the hallway. In a whispering tone he said, "Ya know, it doesn't matter how good you are, your reputation can be ruined by a few comments passed along to a few key people. It would be best for you to get with the program."

It's One of the Manager's in My Department

"Hello, Aurora. My name is Arthur Jones. A colleague suggested that I call you. I have a problem among the people my department; I'm not sure if a consultant can help with this kind of thing, but I thought I'd call you anyway."

"Hello, Arthur. I might be able to help, it depends on the problem. Can you tell me a little bit about the problem and how you've approached it so far?"

"Sure. It's one of the managers in my department—his name is Aldo. He seems to want to do his own thing and go his own way. The other managers complain to me all the time about him. I've spoken with him, but it doesn't seem to make a difference."

"How's the quality of his work?"

"His individual work is fine; it's when he works with the other managers as a team that problems surface. He's disruptive and uncooperative; he won't go along with anyone else's suggestions. It's bogging the team down—things are taking longer than necessary to get done. Have you dealt with situations like this?"

"Yes. I have a three stage approach for this kind of problem. First, I interview all the members of the team one-on-one to understand the issue as they see it. Then I interview people outside the team who may be involved or affected. Last, I design a session to work with you and the managers who report to you to get the concerns out in the open in a controlled and safe way, and to clarify points and discuss possible resolutions. Does that sound like something you'd be willing to try?"

"Sure, I'll try anything at this point!"

Aurora was startled to discover that every manager she interviewed, with one exception, said almost exactly the same thing:

"We only have one problem in this group: Aldo. He gets in the way of everything we try to do. He's uncooperative. The rest of us work well together." They would not be more specific.

When she interviewed Aldo, he said, "I'm really concerned about the impact this group is having on the company. They're violating the standards. They're doing work that is going to cause problems down stream. I keep trying to caution them, to warn them that these projects won't work, but they all go along with Arthur. He doesn't care because it makes him look good to get things done quickly and he doesn't have to fix the problems—other departments get stuck with them."

Aurora interviewed the managers in two other departments and discovered that Aldo's charges were justified. She met with Arthur to get his reaction to the information she had uncovered. He said, "I was hoping you could help me get rid of this guy. I never expected this thing to take a turn in this direction. I guess you can't help me after all."

The Gang

"Hello, Adele. If you're still interested in the position, I'd like you to come back for a second interview. This time I'd like you to meet with two of the people you'll be working with since this is their area of specialization and not mine."

"Yes, Emmet, I'm very interested in the position and I'd be glad to meet with the other members of your department."

On the day of the second interview, Emmet said, "Thanks for coming back, Adele. I'd like to introduce you to Denslow and Ursula. They're developing courses in the Executive Education curriculum you'll be working on. You'll be working with them as a team, so I thought it would be a good idea for them to be part of the interview process."

"Hello, I'm pleased to meet you, but I'm curious: Why do you need another person on your team?"

Denslow responded, "Our target date to complete the curriculum has been moved up and Ursula and I won't be able to get all the courses written in time. We need someone who can hit the ground running and develop two of the courses. According to your resume, it looks like you have the expertise we need, so we wanted to meet with you in person."

An hour and a half later, Emmet said, Would you excuse us for a few moments, Adele. The three of us would like to confer. I'll be right back."

When Emmet returned he said, "We all agree. I'd like to offer you the position."

Adele met frequently with Denslow and Ursula to discuss the common themes among the projects they were working on and to ensure that there was no duplication of subject matter. During these meetings, Adele couldn't help but notice that Denslow and Ursula were inexperienced and unqualified in this line of work, and that they were Emmet's personal friends. After Adele completed her two courses, Emmet instructed Adele, Denslow and Ursula to review each other's work. He told them to notice the differences in style, and report on those differences at the next staff meeting.

Adele's mouth fell open when she reviewed the courses Denslow and Ursula had developed. Not only did their courses not teach the concepts they were supposed to teach, but they contained poorly designed exercises, irrelevant and inaccurate information, and stories with no learning points.

Emmet began the meeting, "Adele, why don't you go first. What differences did you notice?"

Aware that Denslow and Ursula had seen the differences between her professional work and their amateur work, she proceeded cautiously, "I see that we use a different voice, introduce business concepts differently, and use headings differently." She did not mention the serious errors she had seen. She waited to hear what they would say first, but they avoided the issue.

Emmet was called away from the meeting early and asked the three team members to continue without him. Denslow said, "I don't think there's anything else to say." He looked at Ursula, and they left together quietly.

Adele started a new project and did not meet with Denslow and Ursula again, but Denslow and Ursula met frequently with Emmet. Adele overheard their conversations and saw Emmet, Denslow and Ursula looking at her material and overheard that they were trying to learn from her work. Then Denslow and Ursula began to rewrite their courses.

One day, Emmet called Adele into his office and said, "Have you noticed the change in the team atmosphere around here?"

"I've noticed that we're not working on the same project now so we don't meet as often."

"Is that all?"

"Pretty much."

"Don't you feel the tension?"

"I'm not working on projects with the others now and, working in my isolated area, I don't get to see them often , so I don't know what's going on with them."

"It's you. You're having a negative effect on the team."

"Me? What have I done?"

"Two people in the department have come to me and complained that you're causing disharmony."

"I'll be glad to meet with them so we can discuss whatever it is they're concerned about and resolve it. I'd like you to be present, though, so there won't be any misinterpretations."

"I'm not going to hold any meetings like that! I want you to just start being polite and courteous to your peers."

"I'm not aware of having been impolite or discourteous to anyone. I'd really like to know exactly what I'm being charged with."

"Just do what I told you to do."

After that meeting, everyone in the department, including Emmet, became openly hostile toward Adele, but they falsely accused her of being hostile toward them. Eventually, Emmet stopped assigning projects to Adele. He said, "Invent something to do—find a topic you'd like to work on and develop a course about it."

While Emmet was out of the office one day, his assistant burst into Adele's workspace and began shouting at her. The assistant blocked Adele's access to the passageway and lunged toward Adele several times, with her arms flailing as if threatening physical harm. Adele couldn't understand what the assistant was saying. Five minutes after she left, Adele walked out into the main hallway and saw the assistant talking with Ursula, trembling and choking, as if pretending to be upset. The assistant accused Adele of having threatened her!

Emmet had used Adele to teach him and his "gang." He never intended for her to stay in the organization. When he thought they had learned enough, he used his cult to build a false case against Adele so he could either terminate her or to make her so miserable that she would resign.

What Cult-Maker Bosses Want from You

Cult-Maker Bosses want you to worship them. They want your blind obedience and allegiance and they want you to go along with the majority without question. They want you to believe their ideas are so creative and innovative that they will lead to fame and fortune. They want you to trust that they will make you an expert in an emerging or evolving field if you'll be loyal to them. They want you to be patient and wait for them to dole out their wisdom, a bit at a time, as a reward for your public demonstrations of loyalty to them. They want you to pretend to understand them even when what they say is vague or illogical.

You are a tool to these bosses to be used to help them do as they please as supreme ruler of their department. They want you to compensate for the lack of skill and knowledge among the employees they hired for loyalty alone, wanting you to teach their groupies, your "peers," without acknowledging that they lack the skills and knowledge necessary to do their job.

Cult-Maker Bosses also want you to protect their "turfdom" from interference by others outside the department. They want you to surround them like a sentry guarding a revered prophet and collect information about anything that has the potential to threaten their reign. They want you to scorn people who question their ideas and actions and drive those people out of their "turfdom." They want you to help them convince others that their knowledge is so superior that the organization is lucky to have them.

Reporting to a Cult-Maker Boss

Unless you blindly worship your manager, reporting to a Cult-Maker Boss is like being a "Cinderella" or "Cinderfella," living in servitude to a nasty stepmother and spoiled stepsisters. No matter how hard you work or how good you are at what you do, you are not acknowledged by your Cult-Maker Boss, but he or she raves about your coworker's insignificant accomplishments.

Cult-Maker Bosses make you doubt the things you have seen them do and heard them say. They don't respond to your questions with direct answers—they react by asking their own questions to divert you from your original topic. Cult-Maker Bosses speak vaguely when instructing employees, leaving their meaning open to interpretation. When they do "accidentally" give you a direct instruction, if you quote them, they weasel out of their meaning claiming they were speaking metaphorically or giving you a guideline rather than an instruction. They are quick to challenge the words you use to say things, and they make you paraphrase yourself until your statements are diluted to the point of being unworthy of discussion. They laugh at you or make fun of you when you speak intelligently or contribute useful ideas.

Cult-Maker Bosses require you to obtain their approval before you discuss your work with people in other departments, and they prohibit you from talking with certain people, insisting that you communicate through them. They discredit you with people outside your department, and encourage those people to interact directly with her or him instead of you.

THE CULT-MAKER BOSS SURVIVAL QUIZ

Examine your relationship with your Cult-Maker Boss objectively in this "True-or-False" quiz:

Statement:	T	F
1. You do not mind that your boss excludes you from meetings with your peers.		
2. You do not mind that your boss socializes with some of your peers but gives the impression that you are not welcome.		
3. It is okay with you that you are the only person in your group who understands the theories and principles of its work.		
4. You are not distracted from your point when someone in authority challenges what you say and how you say it.		
5. You are comfortable and remain confident when your perspective differs from others.		
6. You do not mind your boss criticizing you in front of the people who use your work.		
7. You are comfortable communicating through your boss or a coworker with the people who receive your completed work.		
8. You are willing to accept blame for problems caused by your boss and/or your coworkers.		

If you are not one of your Cult-Maker Boss's groupies and you responded "<u>True</u>" to most of these statements, there is a good chance that you might survive reporting to a Cult-Maker Boss longer than most, but not without experiencing negative consequences. Your Cult-Maker Boss will continually bombard your character and eventually wear you down.

If you responded "<u>False</u>" to two or more of the statements in the Cult-Maker Boss Survival Quiz, then it is very likely that you are already experiencing negative effects from your current position.

Strategies for Surviving Your Cult-Maker Boss

If you do not fit the "blind follower" mold and cannot or will not satisfy your Cult-Maker Boss's wants, then there is little you can do to survive this reporting relationship unharmed. Look for another job and consider the following strategies for as long as you continue to report to your Cult-Maker Boss:

- Conceal your knowledge about your Cult-Maker Boss's charade; pretend you are unaware of her or his incompetence.

- Do not respond when your Cult-Maker Boss criticizes you, tries to devalue you or twists your words; a display of either confidence or insecurity will trigger more berating.

- Verify all project requirements that your boss and/or coworkers pass on to you, even if you are prohibited from speaking with others—do it secretly.

- Keep track of your completed work to be certain that it isn't altered or presented as someone else's work when it reaches its users.

- Be aware that your Cult-Maker Boss is most likely using your co-workers to make you the scapegoat for dysfunction in your department.

- Don't say anything to your co-workers that you wouldn't want your boss to know.

- Be especially aware of co-workers who ask you many questions but share little about themselves; their feigned friendship may be an attempt to gain your trust so you won't suspect them of being part of your boss's collusive cult.

- Be aware of co-workers who seem overly friendly with you in one-on-one situations but exclude you from group discussions.

- Secretly establish professional contacts with people in other departments to build a reputation as a competent contributor to your organization, and get to know people you might list as references if you decide to leave the organization.

These strategies will only help you slowdown a Cult-Maker Boss's attempts to brainwash or ostracize you—you cannot stop her or him.

Strategies That Won't Work

Don't even think about trying to talk to a Cult-Maker Boss about your concerns about the work environment—he or she will try to convince you that it's all in your head. Your attempt to discuss issues will only alert your boss that you are onto her or him, and then the floodgates of fury will open up upon you.

You will be ostracized for escalating your concerns to your boss's manager or to the Human Resource Department. It is most likely that your boss has already prohibited you from talking with anyone else in the organization without first getting her or his approval, so seeking help outside the department makes you automatically guilty of insubordination—just as your boss planned it. If you are new to the organization, you have no credibility yet, and your boss will be invited into the conversation anyway. Remember that Cult-Maker Bosses are charismatic, smooth-talkers; they can sweep your agenda out from under your feet in an instant and suddenly your meeting will be about *your* inappropriate behavior even if you boss has to invent charges against you.

Even if you have worked at your organization for a long time and have established a fine reputation in other departments, you are still at a disadvantage. Your Cult-Maker Boss is recognized by management as the new prophet of your industry—the one who knows things that no one else knows and who will introduce changes that will save your company. Even though this is bogus, you will come across as a resistor to change.

If you have been one of your Cult-Maker Boss's loyal followers and then you suddenly see the light and want to disassociate yourself from your boss, that's probably not going to happen. You are already guilty of collusion, so you've left a trail of mediocre or less than adequate work behind that your boss will use against you. Secretly search for another job while trying not to let your boss know that you are unhappy or dissatisfied.

Interview Strategies

What to listen for:

- An articulate speaker with overly ambitious plans for the department.
- Emphasis on producing products and services in untried ways of her or his invention.
- Extremely negative criticism of competitors, spoken sarcastically.
- Unwillingness to discuss commonly-understood principles of the type of work done in the department.
- Heavy emphasis on the team environment of the group or department.
- Involving people in your interview who will be your co-workers

Any one of these signs by itself is not a great concern—it is the combination of several of them that you are looking for.

In addition to these signs, be alert for indications that this boss thinks you would add a completely different dimension to the department and stimulate others to do things differently. If your skills and knowledge are completely different, there is a good chance that you are being considered as an unofficial teacher for an incompetent workgroup and manager, and you are likely to be used and tossed away.

Accepting the Consequences of Staying

Cult-Maker Bosses may just be passing through their current assignment on the way to bigger and better things, but they're going to leave a wake in their path. If you choose to stay with a Cult-Maker Boss but do not become a loyal follower and co-conspirator in her or his "innovator" scam, your situation will become increasingly worse. Expect to be blamed for more and more for the dysfunction in your department. Also expect your boss's and coworkers' hostility to increase steadily. You may develop a stress-related health disorder in this situation. Monitor your personal behavior and consumption carefully. Be aware of overindulgence in substances of any kind (especially food, alcohol, pharmaceuticals and other mood-altering consumables)—this can be a clue that your time to move on may have already passed.

Your decision to continue to report to a Cult-Maker Boss is not really a choice in the long term. Sooner or later you will be forced to either become your boss's disciple or leave the organization.

11: THE PILFERER

"It's mine to use as I want!"

How to Recognize a Pilferer Boss

"Where's Jerome?" the new sales associate asked.

"I'm taking messages for him" replied his secretary.

"I need to ask him some questions about my first few meetings with potential clients."

"I'll let him know."

"I need to talk to him today—I have a follow-up meeting with a potential client tomorrow morning. Will that be possible?"

"I don't know. I'll ask him."

"How will you ask him if he's not here?"

"I'll call him on his cell."

"Can I have that number so I can call him myself and save some time?"

"No, I can't give it out."

"Why not?"

"He told me not to."

"Not even to me? I haven't had any training—he said he'd be available to answer questions, but every time I call or look for him, he's not around."

"Maybe one of the Senior Associates can help you. Freda's in the back office, do you want to talk to her?"

"Sure."

"Hi, Freda, would you mind if I asked you a few technical questions?"

"I think Jerome would want to work with you himself because you're so new."

"But Jerome's never around when I need him, and his secretary won't give me his number. Do you know how to reach him?"

"She won't give you the number? Then he must be working at is wife's business today."

"How can he get away with that?"

"Headquarters is four states away."

Pilferer Bosses take privileges and assets they're not entitled to at the expense of their organization. They are often mysteriously unavailable during large blocks of business hours while they secretly attend to personal matters or another business with which they are affiliated. Some own a business of their own, in addition to being an employee at their organization, and work on their own business matters while collecting a salary from the organization that employs them. Others take assets from their organization to enhance their personal lifestyle or to benefit their family members and friends. On the job, they spend company funds on inappropriate, unneeded and poor quality products and/or services to gain personal favor with vendors.

Pilferer Bosses don't always conceal all their actions from employees, but they do cover their tracks. They strike out at employees who question them and launch preemptory attacks against employees who know enough to expose their wrongdoings. They spread rumors about their employees' honesty and integrity to make those employees appear to be likely suspects in the event that losses incurred due to the Pilferer Boss's misdeeds are discovered and investigated.

Pilferer Bosses behave as though they believe it is their right to take from their employer whatever they can get away with. They expect that others do the same, or would do the same, if they had the chance. Their game is to take all they can get and to get away with more than anyone else. They pride themselves on their cunning and their ability to fool the people they report to.

From a Pilferer Boss's point of view, how much a person gets away with is an indication of how smart he or she is. Pilferer Bosses accuse people who do not take advantage of the assets and privileges to which they have access of being foolish or stupid for not doing so. Pilferer Bosses judge character based on whether a person is clever enough not to get caught at being dishonest—not based on honesty or integrity, attributes which are seen as ignorance and/or weakness by Pilferer Bosses.

Pilferer Bosses also lie and cheat in the conduct of business for the organization that employs them to bring in more business but under false pretenses. Then they use those results to rationalize that they deserve more compensation and privileges than they already receive. They refer to these "successes" as justification for their misappropriations. You might hear them say things such as:

- "When you accomplish as much as I do, you're entitled to special privileges"

- "Everyone lies, cheats, and steals, and we all know it."

These statements are nothing more than rationalizations for their behavior.

Pilferer Examples

The Questionable Expenses

Dinah reviewed her training department's monthly budget as soon as it arrived. She noticed a charge of almost $2,000 that she hadn't authorized. Her investigation led her to discover that the unauthorized charge coincided with one of her Vice President's trips. She approached him and asked,

"Charlie, did you charge this dinner party to my budget?"

"I may have."

"I'd like to transfer it out because it's not a training expense, but I'm not sure which account to transfer it into; it's not covered under company policy. Did you get a special authorization for it?"

Charlie clenched his jaw, took a deep, slow breath and hissed through stiffened lips,

"What gives *you* the right to question *me*? What's wrong with your personality that you would even attempt to question me?"

"*What*? You hired me to manage this department's operations and budget. That's what I'm doing."

"Yeah, but I never expected this."

"You never expected what?"

"I never expected to find *intelligence*!"

Dinah stood frozen and didn't respond. She wondered: *Did he hire me because he thought I was dumb?*

Charlie continued, "Give it to my secretary. Tell her to transfer it into this account…"

The tension between Charlie and Dinah heightened as the weeks passed and Dinah discovered more inappropriate charges to her budget. Charlie wouldn't talk to her about these issues, and she was going to be held accountable, so she sent e-mail messages to him to establish some documentation that would indicate she had tried to investigate these questionable expenses if anyone ever challenged her integrity. When the tension became intolerable, she decided to get help from Charlie's boss, Travis, who responded,

"Charlie told me about you. He said you were a problem person. I guess he was right."

"I'm only trying to do my job."

"But you're upsetting your boss."

"My boss is upsetting *me*. That's why I'm here. I need your help."

"Here' my advice: STOP IT!'"

"Stop what?"

"Stop telling him whatever it is you're telling him that gets him so upset."

"But…"

"Just listen; this is all I'm going to say to you: your relationship with your boss is *your* problem; *you* fix it! Don't question him—find a way to keep him from getting upset with you."

In that moment, Dinah realized how pervasive the problem was in this company.

The Squandered Investment

Hazel convinced her Senior VP that she could save the company hundreds of thousands of dollars a year with a $2.6 million investment, so she was promoted. Her former peers, who had disapproved her ideas with strong support to back them up, now reported to her. At her first meeting with them, she said,

"There'll be no more paperwork around here. We're going to throw away our existing documents. Everything will be electronically developed and stored."

One of the managers asked, "How will employees get access to information? They don't have the necessary technology."

"Leave it to me. I'm bringing in a vendor I've worked with in the past. They're experts at this."

Another manager asked, "Will they be working with us?"

"No, they're going to provide the infrastructure. For now, you'll continue to oversee the completion of the projects your people are currently working on. Once the infrastructure is in place, you'll all be trained to use it."

"How will the vendors know what we need?"

"I'm bringing in a consultant to do a study."

"A consultant? How will you find someone knowledgeable about our processes? Are you going to put these jobs out for bids?"

"No. I'm hiring people I've worked with in the past."

Two months later, when the consultant made her presentation, several of the managers questioned the findings. Hazel jumped in and said, "Look, these are the facts and we're going ahead with these recommendations. These are not just my ideas anymore, they've been validated by this study and I don't want to hear anymore objections. You're all too entrenched in your old ways to appreciate where we need to go."

Then the technology-infrastructure consultants arrived—another of Hazel's former acquaintances. They designed the technological capability without talking to any of the managers. When the managers voiced their concerns about not providing input into the process, Hazel said, "Okay, you want to be involved? I'm going to hire a management consultant to be my coach. He'll help me make sure that I include your ideas."

Hazel held a meeting to introduce her "coach," Harris, to the managers. She seemed like a completely different person when Harris was around: she spoke in softened tones; her face was pink; she tilted her head and bounced her hair; she smiled and stared at him when he spoke, like an infatuated teenager.

Harris said to the group of managers, "I'm here to help Hazel be a better manager. She knows you have some concerns, and I'm here to facilitate between you and her—to make sure your opinions are acknowledged. Do you have any questions for me?"

One manager asked, "What's your background?"

"I was a technician in this business. When I was laid off, I became a Management Consultant. Hazel was my first client. She hired me while she worked at the company that laid me off. Since then, I've consulted to her in the other companies she's worked in."

"What are your credentials for this kind of work?"

"I didn't go to college, if that's what you mean. I'm self-taught. I've read a lot of books and attended professional workshops. And I have other clients who can attest to my work."

Harris conducted meetings regularly with this group of managers and wrote their concerns on charts. Then he would say: "I'll be working privately, one-on-one with Hazel about these issues." Hazel was always "sweet" when speaking to her managers in Harris's presence, but when he was not there she resorted to her forceful and abrupt behavior. After each meeting, she chastised the managers, saying on one occasion: "You people need to show Harris more respect! I brought him in to help *you*!"

While Harris was collecting the managers' concerns, the technology consultants were busy developing the new system—without input from the managers. When the budgeted money was spent, the project was still incomplete, but Hazel implemented it anyway. Employees refused to use the new system because it didn't contain the information they needed. Hazel had successfully financed her friends' businesses, thereby retaining their loyalty and camaraderie, but at great cost to her employer.

A Permanent Friday Afternoon

Helga reassured Flynn during his first day on the job: "If I'm not around, you can always reach me by e-mail, cell phone or instant messaging (IM). Or you can talk to Gina—she's been here for a while and I've asked her to be available to you."

Flynn got right to work and didn't have any questions until Friday afternoon. He couldn't proceed without additional information about his project. Helga wasn't in her office, so he called her cell phone number and left a message. An hour later, he sent an e-mail message and an instant message. No response. Two and half hours later, Helga called him:

"Sorry I didn't get back to you right away; I got involved in something on my computer and didn't check my messages."

"I sent you an IM, didn't it come up on your screen?"

"I'm working on a different computer. What do you need?"

Flynn was frustrated that so much time had been wasted, but being new, he didn't want his frustration to show. During the next week, Helga was available to Flynn and quickly responded when he left messages for her. He chalked up the first incident as an unusual occurrence until he noticed a pattern—Helga was never available on Friday afternoons and some mornings he couldn't reach her until after 10:00. He contacted Gina on those occasions as Helga had instructed him to do:

"Hi Gina; got a minute?"

"Sure, what's up?"

"I'm having trouble with this in-house system. It won't accept my text. Can you tell me what I need to do?"

While Gina was examining his text, Flynn said, "I'm really sorry to bother you but Helga said you wouldn't mind."

"No, I don't mind. I usually cover for her when she's not around."

"Where is she when she's not around?"

"I don't know. Meetings, I guess…There it is—the system doesn't accept this punctuation; you have to tag it—like this…"

"Thanks for your help."

"You're welcome."

During a lunch conversation, several of Flynn's colleagues talked about web site designs they thought were particularly well done. Gary said, "Did you see the one I developed for Helga?"

"You mean the department web site?" Flynn asked.

"No, the one I developed for her business. She and her husband have a consulting business on the side. They contracted me to develop it for them. Their site is really cool!"

One month later, Helga said, I'll be out of town and unreachable next week. Let's discuss what you're all going to do during that time and what resources you'll need in my absence."

Without thinking, Flynn blurted out, "Don't worry, we'll do just fine—it'll be like a permanent Friday afternoon."

Helga sat up straight in her chair. She and Gina quickly exchanged glances. Then, with a flat grin and in a sing-song voice, Helga said, "That's not nice."

What Pilferer Bosses Want from You

Pilferer bosses want you to overlook their indiscretions. They want you to pretend that you don't see them take things and/or privileges to which they are not entitled, to help them gain access to things they can use to their personal advantage, and to ignore their unwise and inappropriate expenditures of company funds. They want you to cover for them when they are unavailable and unreachable, whether or not you know where they are and what they are doing. They want you to keep quiet about the things they do; they don't want to discuss them with you and they don't want you to discuss those things with anyone else, either.

Pilferer Bosses want you to take things from your organization, too, with their knowledge and approval. But they want you to do it on a much smaller scale than they do—you should not benefit more than they do. By following their example and taking whatever you want, you provide Pilferer Bosses with insurance that you will not snitch on them—they have something on you. Any "trust" you perceive in your relationship with your boss is fake— there is no trust among thieves. As soon as you begin to take things you're not entitled to from your organization, you become your boss's competitor in her or his eyes, even though he or she encouraged you.

Reporting to a Pilferer Boss

Reporting to a Pilferer boss is like being a suspect in a crime with an unethical investigator searching for evidence against you, as if he or she is certain you are guilty. The more straightforward you are, the more your Pilferer Boss suspects you of committing the same dishonest acts he or she commits. It is almost incomprehensible to Pilferer Bosses that an honest person can actually exist in our society.

Pilferer bosses expect everyone to behave dishonestly. Because they do it, they expect everyone else to be guilty of the same or similar acts. They set traps to test your honesty, pretending to trust you with assets for short periods of time while they closely monitor your actions. They quietly sneak up on you while you're doing your job, as if they expect to catch you in the act of doing something inappropriate. They monitor your phone calls, e-mail messages, Internet usage and conversations secretly, but not to terminate you—they are looking for bargaining power to use against you when and if you catch them in a dishonest act. They will use whatever they find out about you, no matter how insignificant (like a company pen in your appointment book, pocket or purse), to demonstrate that you are no different than they are.

Unless you are in cahoots with your boss, he or she is most likely setting you up as a suspect in the event that losses resulting from her or his misdeeds are uncovered. For this reason, other people in your organization probably distrust *you*, and you may not be aware of that.

Pilferer Bosses are often unavailable and mysteriously unreachable when you need them. They prepare you in advance for their undisclosed absences with statements such as:

- "If you need me, leave a message. Don't try to find me."

- "If anyone you don't know calls, just take a message for me—don't try to help."

Pilferer Bosses may force you to ignore your commitments to your organization's goals by reassigning you to work on projects that benefit them personally, such as doing things for their house, family, or another business they own or in which they have a financial interest.

When you ask Pilferer Bosses about what they're doing, they become hostile and yell, sneer, threaten, and/or counter-challenge you. They create a flap of noise and motion to disorient you; then they change the subject and redirect your attention to your own shortcomings—real or fabricated. They also threaten to damage your professional reputation, if they haven't done so already. When they are challenging you or think that you are challenging them, they may say things such as:

- "You ask too many questions. Just do your job."

- "You don't know what I do when I'm not here."

- "What I do is none of your business."

- "Things aren't always what they appear to be."

- "Make sure you have all you're facts straight before you make accusations."

Whether you are new to your organization or have been working there for a while, Pilferer Bosses treat employees in the same way—everyone is eligible to become a suspect for their misdeeds. If you pride yourself on your integrity, reporting to a Pilferer Boss will be difficult for you.

The Pilferer Boss Survival Quiz

Examine your relationship with your Pilferer Boss objectively in this "True-or-False" quiz:

Statement:	T	F
1. You are comfortable accepting your company's assets as gifts from your boss.		
2. You think it is appropriate for your boss to secretly grant you undeserved privileges.		
3. It is okay with you that your boss purchases unneeded and/or poor quality products or services to get personal favors.		
4. You think it is appropriate for your boss to be absent and unaccounted for during business hours.		
5. It doesn't bother you that your boss charges inappropriate expenses to the organization.		
6. You are comfortable making excuses for your boss to conceal her or his indiscretions.		
7. You do <u>not</u> care that your boss says things about you which cause others to suspect you of being dishonest or untrustworthy.		
8. You don't mind taking the blame for your boss's dishonest acts.		

If you responded "True" to most of these statements, then there is a good chance that you might survive reporting to a Pilferer Boss without experiencing too much negative stress, but not without suffering some of the effects of a guilty conscience or feeling like an accomplice. You cannot hide your awareness of inappropriate behavior from yourself without creating internal stress.

If you responded "False" to two or more of these statements and you report to a Pilferer Boss, then it is very likely that you are already experiencing negative effects from your current position, or that you are unaware that trouble is looming in the background waiting for you.

Strategies for Surviving Your Pilferer Boss

If you are unwilling to become your boss's "partner in crime," then you will need to protect yourself from being blamed for your boss's misdeeds. Consider the following strategies:

- Expect your boss to set you up to take blame for her or his misuse of the organization's assets, and leave a clearly documented trail for all of your actions.

- Carefully monitor any assets you are responsible for overseeing, and verify that all uses and authorizations are valid. Make it standard practice for everyone to provide documentation related to use of assets.

- Put in writing all communications with your boss regarding use of assets and save hard copies of those written records in a secure location.

- Politely refuse gifts of company property and special privileges, but do not mention ethical issues as reasons for your refusal; in an upbeat way, say that you don't need or want special privileges for doing your job.

- Suspect that if your boss is getting away with misuse and misappropriation of assets then her or his manager may also be guilty; escalating your concerns may put you at greater risk if that is the case.

- Do not become friendly with vendors your boss deals with; maintain a strictly professional relationship and discuss only the project at hand.

- When your boss is mysteriously absent, delay the resolution of problems that require her or his involvement until he or she returns. Do not contact other managers to substitute for your boss during these absences.

- If you are concerned that your boss might be unreachable when you need a signature for an urgent or time-critical matter, ask your boss to arrange in advance for another manager to be on "standby" for this purpose. Explain that doing so would be in the best interest of your organization's goals.

- If someone inquires about your boss's whereabouts when he or she is unreachable, offer to assist that person rather than answer their question. If anyone insists on an answer, simply say: "I don't know where he or she is at the moment" (if that is the truth) and leave it at that.

- If your boss explicitly asks you to lie for her or him, say you are uncomfortable being placed in that position and ask for an alternative that is acceptable to both of you.

- Examine your responsibility as a silent witness to your Pilferer Boss's inappropriate behavior and acknowledge the ethical dilemma this creates for you. Don't try to fool yourself into accepting this behavior as appropriate.

Strategies That Won't Work

Reporting your boss's behavior to a higher level manager could be risky, especially if your boss does little to hide her or his misdeeds. It is highly likely that corruption permeates the ranks of your organization's hierarchy, and employees who threaten to expose management for taking undeserved assets and privileges become the targets of organized harassment within their hierarchy.

Trying to explain to your boss the consequences of her or his actions will not work, either. Your boss is well aware of who is bearing the cost of her or his indiscretions. Pilferer Bosses rationalize that they deserve the things they take, considering those things part of the compensation owed to them; you cannot convince them otherwise.

A discussion about religious beliefs won't work, either; this topic will probably be prohibited. Pilferer Bosses will tell you to keep your personal beliefs out of the workplace. You cannot "save" Pilferer Bosses or help them save themselves from the consequences of their actions.

Interview Strategies

What to listen for:

- Questions about your values—both direct and indirect.
- Extreme emphasis on learning the details of your past mistakes.
- Probing about how you handled situations in which your boss was wrong in the past.

A good boss may ask these same questions, but heavy emphasis in these areas may indicate a Pilferer Boss.
If you suspect that the person you are interviewing with is a Pilferer Boss, casually mention that you are looking for an organization with standards that are compatible with your values. If asked for examples, discuss a boss you reported to in the past but do not mention the company name or the boss's name. A Pilferer Boss might not offer you the job if you make values a high priority, so you could avoid a bad situation by using this strategy.

Accepting the Consequences of Staying

Tolerating your boss's unethical behavior is like giving her or him your approval, and that makes you an accomplice. You cannot rationalize this away. Your organization's assets belong to its investors or owners, and you are watching your boss steal from those people and doing nothing about it. If you are bothered by this situation now, recognize that it will only get worse. Pilferer Bosses control their environment and the people in it—that includes you. Sooner or later, you are going to be coerced to become a more active participant in one your boss's scams against your organization. The longer you stay, the harder it will become for you to resist the pressure. It may go on for years.

If your boss is eventually caught, employees who cooperated with her or him, or did nothing to expose her or his dishonesty, may be let go, too, and will certainly be mistrusted.

If your values say "no" while your actions say "yes," this tension will begin to affect other areas of your life, such as your relationships or your health.

12: THE SABOTEUR

"I can make it look like I support this change!"

How to Recognize a Saboteur Boss

Many of the engineers in one large company would become eligible for retirement within the next five years. The Human Resource Department recruited high-achieving college graduates into a program designed to transfer knowledge and expertise from the experienced engineers to these new engineers who would succeed them. The new engineers were assigned to Engineering Managers who would become their mentors and be responsible for teaching them.

One year after they were recruited, the new engineers attended a leadership workshop together. During one of the lessons, the facilitator asked, "What do you expect from your career?" The young employees called out answers, one after the other:

- "Not much!"
- "Money and power!"
- "Headaches!"
- "Oppression!"

Surprised by these responses, the facilitator said, "These don't sound like very optimistic expectations. You've been specially chosen to work in an advanced program. You have advantages that most people don't get. What's going on?"

"Advantages! I'll tell you what's special about this program: we get to be jerked around by a bunch of old guys."

"What old guys? Are you talking about your mentors?"

"Mentors?! You must be kidding! These guys aren't teaching us anything! They're using us for their entertainment. We get stupid little clerical assignments. They don't explain things to us; they don't even let us go to project meetings to find out what's going on. In staff meetings, they set us up to make presentations but they give us wrong information to present and then they ridicule us in front of the entire group."

"How many of you are having this problem?"

Seventeen hands went up from this group of 22.

"Have any of you reported this to your Human Resource advisors?"

"Yeah; they're useless. They tell us we have to learn to get along with our managers, that it's part of business life and we shouldn't expect things to be like they were in school!"

"They don't help?"

"Oh, yeah, they help. They've reassigned half of us to different mentors."

"That's good, isn't it?"

"Nope. It just starts all over again with the new person."

"Hmm. Yet you're all still here. Why?"

"Because this company has a good reputation and if we can get at least two or three years experience on our resume it'll look good when we apply at other companies."

At the break, the facilitator checked with the Human Resource Manager who oversaw this recruitment program. After explaining what the new employees had said, she asked, "Are you aware of this?"

"Yes."

"Well what's going on?"

"I think the managers are only pretending to go along with the program. Before I met with them one day, I overheard several of them talking about how *they* had to learn the *hard* way, and how they'll be darned if they're gonna hand over their knowledge on a silver platter to a bunch of kids."

Saboteur Bosses say they support their organization's goals and programs, but they either blatantly or surreptitiously work against those plans. They defy any change to the status quo, including changes in technology, methods, business strategy, organization design, and culture.

Some Saboteurs are afraid they're going to be blocked from taking assets and privileges they aren't entitled to if new programs are implemented; some are "retired-in-place" and just don't want to be bothered learning new ways to conduct business; and others want the organization to use their ideas instead so they can receive recognition and rewards.

Saboteur Bosses misdirect and misinform the people who report to them so that those employees will do things that make the organization's new goals and programs appear ineffective. They focus on the shortcomings of new programs, and they offer no constructive criticism or suggestions for improvement. They advocate for a return to the old ways.

Saboteur Bosses may have stopped learning, developing skills and contributing to their organization long ago, yet they expect to continue to collect a salary as a reward for their earlier accomplishments while offering nothing new in return. They dwell in the past, talking about the way things were and emphasizing how much harder it was to work back when they began their career. They criticize new methods and techniques saying they diminish the profession by requiring little or no skill to perform the job, when, in fact, their profession is becoming cross-disciplined and new technical or behavioral skills are required. They ridicule anyone who has not learned "the hard way" or experienced the "old" way of doing things.

Some Saboteur Bosses resent that new goals or programs are someone else's idea and not their own. They intend to prove that their idea is better by doing anything they can to cause new goals or programs to appear inadequate. They see themselves as unsung heroes who know better than anyone else what their organization needs, even though they don't understand the bigger picture of their organization's needs, purpose, challenges and strategy. Their perspective is narrow and focused more on internal, short-term efficiency than on external, long-term effectiveness. They seek acknowledgement and rewards for their ideas, and consider others who receive such acknowledgement as competitors who undeservedly take from them the rewards they believe they are owed. They do not think through their ideas completely, and they do not identify or assess the shortcomings and risks associated with their ideas. They have a different opinion about what their organization should do and they try to prove any new program wrong as a last ditch effort to implement their own plan.

Saboteur Boss Examples

The Bonus

Jason's boss approached him, saying, "We need someone to lead an interdepartmental team to solve the problems associated with this new offering. You've been requested. Will you do it?"

"Me? I tried to prevent those problems from happening in the first place and they wouldn't listen to me. *Now* they want *me* to *fix* them?"

"That's right. Consider it a compliment. You're the best person to help resolve these issues, and they recognize that now."

"What'll I have to do?"

"Don't rub their faces in it. Talk to Alan. You'll report to him temporarily."

Jason met with Alan that afternoon.

"…This is a critical project, Jason. Future offerings are planned as add-ons, and our customers are screaming for us to rip the basic service out—they're ready to go to the competition. We have to fix it. You can pick anyone you want to work on this team—you'll have my full support in getting them reassigned. I've even arranged for a Quality Consultant to work on the team with you. Will you do it?"

"Yes. When do I start?"

"Great! Start assembling the team right now. The first thing I'll need from you after you get the team assembled is an estimate of how long it will take to fix the problems."

Jason convened the first team meeting two weeks later. After introductions, he told the team members:

"Our first task is to estimate how long it's going to take to complete this assignment. We've got to identify all the problems, figure out what needs to be done, fix the existing services, develop new implementation plans and train everyone across all departments."

One of the team members said, "We're going to have to start at the beginning and rework the entire design to fix this mess—we can't just modify the existing program. We have to begin as if we're a newly created project team and design this offering from scratch."

"I understand. The question is: How long will that take?"

The team estimated that it would take ten months; they would finish their work in April. Jason reported this estimate to Alan.

"April! No, it can't take ten months, that's ridiculous. You've got the best experts on your team. Get it done in less time."

"But the best experts estimated that this is the amount of time we need to get it done right, and the Quality Consultant you assigned to work with us supports our decision."

"Go back to the team and recalculate this estimate."

Jason and the experts on his team started over. When they were finished, Jason took the news to Alan:

"We threw out our original work and started over. No matter how we looked at it, we couldn't cut any part of the process—that's how this problem was created in the first place. It's going to take ten months."

"Perhaps you didn't understand me. This project needs to be completed in this calendar year. You've got six months."

"Six months! That's impossible. In six months we'll just be designing the new implementation plan—new orders will still have problems. Why six months?"

Alan responded unashamedly, "I need to report the completion of this project to my management in the current calendar year so I can get bonus and this is the only project in my department that's important enough to qualify for one."

The Unequal Employment Opportunity

Pacing in tight circles and puffing his small, dingy office full of cigar smoke, Efrem barked, "All right, so here you are. Why do you want to meet with me?"

"I'm having a problem with my boss and I need your help" replied Alva.

"What do you mean: *'You're having a problem with your boss'*? That's not the way it works around here; bosses have problems their people. I'm your boss's boss—I have problems with *him*, he doesn't have problems with *me*, get it? You're probably gonna think you have a problem with me, too. We're just not used to having women around here. I'm probably gonna say things you don't like, so don't you mind if I say 'son-of-a-bitch!'"

"Not as long as you don't you mind if I say 'son-of-a-bitch' right back to you!"

Efrem broke out of his pacing circle, turned to face Alva like a soldier coming to attention, and took a step closer to where she was sitting. "So you think you have a problem with your boss, eh? Let me hear it."

"He's teaching me all wrong. He tells me to do things that are incorrect, so all my jobs fail—they bounce back and my peers correct them."

"You're imagining…"

"No, I'm not imagining it."

"What makes you so sure?"

"I noticed that when the technicians would bring jobs back into the office to one of my peers, they would look at me, whisper and laugh. I started color-coding my jobs so I could recognize them. When I see one, I approach the technician and ask what the problem is."

"Good for you. You fix your own mistakes now."

"No, I haven't made any mistakes. I do each job exactly as I'm instructed, and they're bouncing back—they don't work."

"You probably just misunderstood. We don't expect you to get it right away. This is men's work, it's gonna take time to learn it—it's not easy. That's the problem with this damned new policy of putting women in men's jobs…"

"No, I didn't misunderstand…"

"What makes you so sure?"

"I write down exactly what he tells me to do for each job. I keep a copy of his instructions with a copy of the job. When the technician tells me what's wrong, I compare the job to the instructions—and they always match. Then I take the failed job to my boss and pretend it's a new one. He gives me a different set of instructions every time. They never work."

"That's ridiculous. Why would he do a thing like that and why are you trying to make this my problem?"

"I think he wants to make it look like I can't do the job so he can prove to management that it's a mistake to promote women into these positions. It's costing the company money. Every job I do has to be redone. He doesn't seem to care about that and I thought you would."

"You say you've written down all of his instructions?"

"Yes."

"Well, I don't think you're right and I don't think you deserve special treatment, but here's what I'm gonna do. I'm gonna assign another manager to your group. He'll work along side your boss but his only job will be to teach you. Then we'll see if your jobs bounce back. If they do, then it's you; if they don't, then we'll see. How's that sound?"

"I'm not asking for special treatment, I'm just asking to be given a fair chance—to be trained properly, just like everyone else who comes into this job…"

Alva then got the appropriate training—the same training the men in her department received. Her jobs never bounced back again. Within the year, she was transferred to another department.

The Quick Way of Getting It Done

"Hi, Gavin. I'm calling about the results of the Performance-Management audit for your department."

"Hi Sarina. How'd we do?"

"Well, it's not good news, Gavin."

"I can take it—go ahead."

"Your employee satisfaction scores are even lower this year than they were last year."

"I don't understand why. What are they complaining about?"

"I wouldn't call it complaining. They've made some serious charges about the lack of support."

"What kind of support?"

"It's a long list. I think it would be better to meet with you and go over the results in person. When would be a good time?"

"There's no good time around here for stuff like this. We're always putting out fires here. Can't you just tell me over the phone?"

"It's a long list. Are you sure you want to do this over the phone?"

"Yeah, anything that'll save time. Hit me with it."

"It's everything in the Performance Management program. I'll give you the list first, and then we'll discuss each topic in detail, okay?"

"Okay."

"Here's the gist of it:
- There aren't any organizational goals or directions;
- They're given assignments that they're not trained to do;
- The only feedback they get is negative criticism; and
- They haven't had appraisals in over two years."

"Well, they're right. I have no time for that stuff and neither do my managers. What's the fix; what do I need to do to get beyond this report?"

"The fix is to do the work; follow the program—support the people. That's what the Performance Management Program is all about: supporting the people so they can take care of our customers. If you don't support them, you create a vicious cycle—the work can't get done, business results decline, turnover increases, and you have less and less time available because you're always training new people and fixing problems created by their novice attempts to get jobs done."

"Well, you're right about that: turnover is high here. I can't keep people in these jobs for very long. It's the work they keep throwing at us—it's more than we can handle. We spend a lot of time fixing jobs and can't move on to new ones as fast as they come in. And now they tell me they want me to do some 'people' program! It's just one more task we have no time for—we can't even take care of the customers."

"Gavin, the Performance Management program is a Quality Process. It's intended to solve these problems—that's why it was implemented. It's not additional work, it's what was always in your job description—it just has a different name now."

"Look, help me out here, Sarina. There's got to be a short cut—what's the quick way of getting it done? How do I make it look like I'm meeting these requirements?"

"The quick way is what you're doing now—nothing. There's no short cut. Our investment in our employees is the solution to the kind of business problems you're having."

"Well, let whoever wants to punish me come in here and get these jobs done! I don't have time for that kind of nonsense!"

What Saboteur Bosses Want from You

Saboteur Bosses want you to help them undermine your organization's programs by engaging in sabotage with them or by ignoring their sabotage. They want you to agree with them that their ideas are better than anything anyone else can possibly come up with. They want you to identify problems and oversights in new programs designed to change your organization's offerings, policies, strategy, technology, or operations and tell them about those problems so they can build a case to stop the new plan and revert back to the old way of doing things. They want you to follow their orders without question even when they direct you to do things that contradict your organization's goals. They do not care about the negative effects of their actions or inaction, on customers or other recipients of the organization's services; they care only about themselves. They want you to resist change to help them prove that things are better just the way they are.

Some Saboteur Bosses want you to help them find ways to get access to assets and privileges for their personal use when new programs make it more difficult for them to do so. They'll also be happy if you can provide new opportunities for them to take advantage.

Some want you to admire them but not ask them to do anything. They want you to acknowledge that they should no longer be required to learn new ways of working, but should still get paid for all they've done for the organization in the past. They want you to do whatever work is necessary while they slack off. They want you to appreciate them for having blazed the trails that brought your job into existence.

Then there are those Saboteur Bosses who want you to be impressed with them and tell them how much better their ideas are than the newest programs in your organization. They want you to help them convince upper management that their ideas are better and should be implemented instead of any new program that is being considered or introduced. They want you to help them hide facts about the inadequacies of their ideas and plans when they do get to implement them.

Reporting to a Saboteur Boss

Reporting to a Saboteur Boss who is afraid of losing something due to changes in the way things are done is like being a witness to a crime and being unable to stop it or talk about it; it's like being temporarily paralyzed whenever you want to discuss what you have seen or heard. Your jaw may drop in disbelief when your Saboteur Boss gives you blatant instructions to violate organizational policies and procedures—it's hard to accept that a manager would direct you to violate your organization's improvement programs. The people you tell may not believe you because it is so inconceivable that a manager could get away with working against the organization that employs her or him. Some of the blatantly defiant instructions Saboteur Bosses give may include:

- "Report this project as completed four months early so I can get a bonus."

- "I'll tell you when your work is finished."

- "Don't follow the new guidelines, continue working the old way."

- "If you cooperate with the new program, you'll get an unsatisfactory appraisal from me."

Reporting to a Saboteur Boss who is "retired-in-place" is like living in the past; it can feel like you're an actor in a black-and-white television program broadcast in the 1950s. It's depressing; there's no enthusiasm or pride in the work. These Saboteurs talk down to you and keep you uninformed about what is happening in the organization. They prohibit you from learning about new technologies and methods and from developing new skills. They limit your access to information about changes in your organization. They may say things like this:

- "I do what I want around here, and if you want to work here, you'll have to just go along."

- "You should know how important I am to this organization."

- "Your job wouldn't exist if it wasn't for me and the groundwork I did."

- "You call yourself a professional? You have it easy compared to the way things were when I had your job."

- "You'll never be as good as I was."

- "You'll never know what I've already forgotten about this job."

Reporting to a Saboteur Boss who wants her or his own ideas implemented instead of the organization's new programs is like being in a cold war with everyone else in your organization. This boss tells you only negative things about upper management and boasts about her or his frequent fights with superiors. He or she gives you assignments, but doesn't allow you ask questions about them and doesn't explain their purpose. This boss also gives you instructions that contradict your organization's goals, and he or she may suddenly change those instructions or claim to have given you different instructions after you've completed a significant portion of the job. He or she may then challenge you and make you seem responsible for following her or his bad instructions with statements like:

- "This is not what I told you to do!"
- "Why did you assume that this would be acceptable?"
- "Where did you get this information? Show it to me in writing."
- "Don't let anyone find out about what you've done."
- "I'll have to limit your assignments to things I can closely supervise."

The Saboteur Boss Survival Quiz

Examine your relationship with your Saboteur Boss objectively in this "True-or-False" quiz:

Statement:	T	F
1. You do not want your organization to change, not even to challenge competitors.		
2. You don't mind being among the last to know about changes in your organization.		
3. You don't mind that your boss doesn't tell you about things in other departments that may affect your work.		
4. It is okay with you that your boss doesn't explain the reasons for new projects he or she assigns to you.		
5. You are okay with receiving instructions from your boss that contradict your organization's goals.		
6. It doesn't bother you that your boss is outspoken about her or his lack of respect for upper management.		
7. You are comfortable working with outdated technology and don't want to learn new ways of doing your job.		
8. You are willing to let your boss set you up as a bad example to make her or his point.		

If you responded "True" to most of these statements, then there is a good chance that you can survive reporting to a Saboteur Boss without experiencing negative stress, but only in the short term—as long as your boss remains in this job.

If you responded "False" to three or more of these statements, then it is very likely that you are already experiencing negative stress in your current position.

Strategies for Surviving Your Saboteur Boss

You may not be able to prevent your boss from using you to undermine your organization's goals, but there are a few things you can do to slow your boss down or make her or him use someone else first:

- When your Saboteur Boss gives you a new assignment, ask her or him these four questions:

    ○ How does this project fit into our organization's overall strategy?

    ○ Which specific organizational goals does this project support?

    ○ What are the political implications associated with this project?" (In other words who stands to benefit and who stands to lose based on the outcome of the project?)

    ○ What is your interest in this project?

    Explain that you are asking these questions so that you can prioritize your work and document your individual goals and accomplishments accurately.

- Document all instructions you receive from your Saboteur Boss. Then present them to her or him in a memo asking if you understand correctly—do this before you begin work on the project.

- Document your boss's responses to your questions and present them to her or him it as many times as necessary to obtain clarification. Say that you want to be certain you understand correctly, but do not say that the responses contradict the organization's goals.

- Save paper copies of your communications with your boss in a safe place for at least one year after the project is completed.

- If possible, verify all information you receive from your Saboteur Boss with sources you trust and know are reliable.

Eventually, you will either be forced into submission or your situation will become intolerable to both you and your boss. It is best to look for another position on your own early in the relationship rather than waiting for your boss to initiate a transfer or begin to terminate you for false causes. Do not discuss your boss's misdeeds with other managers in the organization if you want to transfer. Make "career development" your reasons for wanting to transfer.

Strategies That Won't Work

Confronting your Saboteur Boss will backfire on you. Saboteur Bosses are likely to laugh at you if you prove to them that they are wrong—they don't care. They are also likely to increase the pressure on you to undermine your organization's goals and serve their personal interests. If you don't like it, they expect you to leave quietly, and they'll support your initiative to transfer or leave as long as you pretend not to notice their misdeeds and do not imply that you can or will expose them.

Escalating your concerns will not work, either. Saboteur Bosses have enough leeway in their jobs to get away with a great deal of inappropriate behavior because their manager may trust them implicitly, may agree with them, may not want to deal with them, or may be incapable of dealing with them. For these reasons, your boss's boss does not want to hear from you—you will be labeled as a trouble maker.

Interview Strategies

What to listen for:

- *We don't always do things the company way in my department.*
- *It doesn't always seem like we're doing the right things, but we are.*

Two questions to ask during an interview to test whether the manager might be a Saboteur Boss are:

- What are the organization's goals and how closely is the work in your department aligned with them?
- What are some of the major changes that have been made in this organization recently and how have you and your employees supported them?

Start a conversation based on the answers to get a sense of the interviewing manager's commitment and loyalty to the organization. An effective manager will be impressed with your questions; a bad boss probably will not hire you, so you will have successfully avoided a bad situation.

Accepting the Consequences of Staying

Your Saboteur Boss will increasingly pressure you to work against your organization's goals and to perform your job in ways that advance her or his ideas for as long as you report to her or him. You will not be able to resist for long. Your Saboteur Boss will isolate you from people who have information about the organization's new programs and will discredit anything you discover on your own. Eventually, you'll be working blindly, following your boss's orders like a robot, without being certain whether you are doing the right thing. Your work will become meaningless to you and you'll have little, if any, sense of pride in it. You'll be working only for the money. This sense of emptiness is likely to affect your personal relationships and your emotional and physical well-being. Counseling can help you in the short term, but it is likely to lead you to accept that you must change your situation before it gets the best of you.

13: THE COMBINATION TYPE

"I never said that!"

How to Recognize Combination Types

What do you do if you've read the descriptions in the previous twelve chapters and you can't quite pinpoint your boss? Or if the twelve types don't *completely* describe your boss? Or if some of the descriptions apply only some of the time? Or if you report to a boss who slips into bad-boss behavior only occasionally? If any of these scenarios describe your situation, then you report to a Combination-Type Boss. This chapter is for you.

Combination-Type Bosses exhibit the behavior of two or more of the bad-boss types described in the previous chapters; however, they do not necessarily exhibit all the behavior associated with any one type. They seem to have Jekyll-Hyde-like personalities; they switch from one mode of behavior to another unpredictably. They appear to be completely different people on different days, and they change their department's goals and employee's instructions to match their shifting moods.

Combination-Type Bosses may occasionally praise employees for accomplishments and then ridicule them for those very same accomplishments on another day. When challenged, they deny having made statements and having given specific instructions as though they have no recollection. They make up explanations as they go along and contradict themselves in the process.

When interacting with their managers, Combination-Type Bosses are stable and act like humble and loyal subordinates—they behave this way consistently in the presence of their superiors. They are quite adept at convincing their superiors to see things their way by somehow convincing their managers that they are doing just what their managers want them to do. They are reactive and immediately make large scale changes in their departments based on subtle suggestions their managers may make or based on inferences they read into their manager's questions. They make frequent changes that last for only short periods of time.

It is quite common for bad bosses to exhibit the behavior of multiple types. To develop a plan for dealing with such a boss, it will be helpful to identify your boss's particular combination of bad-boss types. Follow these two steps:

1. In the previous chapters, flag, underline or highlight sections that describe your boss's behavior.

2. List each of the types that describe some of your boss's behavior here:

This list identifies your boss's "combination type." Don't be surprised if your list includes many types, and don't doubt yourself. You might discover that you report to a Manipulator-Bully Boss, a Suppressor-Confounder-Dumbfounder-Player-Cult Maker Boss, or a Wannabe-Pretender-Propagator-Pilferer-Saboteur Boss—any combination is possible! Bad bosses who exhibit multiple behavior patterns tend to be reactive—they grasp at any method that comes to mind when they're in an awkward situation.

Combination Type Examples

The Special Assignment

Every manager at a higher level than Megan supported her meteoric rise to the upper echelons of the hierarchy. She had the right credentials, the right background, the right contacts and employees who liked her a lot—most of the time.

Sadie acted as the manager for her department temporarily until Megan was formally promoted into the position. When Megan arrived, she was sensitive to Sadie's situation—now displaced by someone new to the department who had no background in this aspect of the business. She said,

"Hello, Sadie. It's nice to meet you. I understand that you've been doing a good job here."

"Hello, Megan. It's nice to meet you, too. I've heard a lot of good things about you, and I'm looking forward to working with you."

"I'm glad to hear that! I understand that this situation must be awkward for you. You've done a good job as the temporary manager here and there's no good reason why you shouldn't have gotten the position. I'm going to need to rely on you to get up to speed. I hope we can work well together."

"I'm sure we will. I've already prepared some information to help you get oriented. Just let me know when you'd like to get started.

Over the next two weeks, Sadie explained the operations of the department and informed Megan of pending matters that needed her approval. During their last orientation meeting, Megan said, "Thank you so much for your help. Now I know why you're a candidate for promotion. You've done an excellent job of making this transition easy for me. I want you to know that I'm the kind of manager who takes care of my people. I want to meet with you next week to discuss your career plans so that I can help you achieve your goals."

Sadie was impressed with Megan, and so were the other managers in the department. They appreciated that she treated them respectfully. But they soon noticed that on some days Megan seemed like a different person—a person no one in the department wanted to know. On her good days, she was a supportive manager; but on her bad days, she could be a Player, a Bully, or a Manipulator. The managers quickly learned to check with Megan's secretary to determine Megan's mood on a particular day before they would talk to her.

When it was time for Megan to prepare performance appraisals, she held a staff meeting. She said playfully, in a sing-song voice, "I have a special assignment for all of you; I'd like you to evaluate each other's performance. Then I'd like to meet with you, one at a time, and hear your reports. This will help me get to know you all a little better and be better informed when I write your appraisals. I'll have my secretary schedule appointments with you— I've got to run now." The managers looked at each other with raised eyebrows as they gathered up their things and quietly went back to their offices.

Sadie was the last manager to meet with Megan. Megan began, "Now that I've heard from all the others, I'm looking forward to hearing your evaluations. Do you have them with you?"

"No, I don't."

"You mean you're not prepared?"

"No. I mean I didn't do the assignment."

Megan sat up straight in her chair and cocked her head to the side as she said in a deepened tone of voice, "Did I hear you right— *you didn't do the assignment?*"

"Yes, that's right."

Squinting her eyes and locking her jaw, Megan asked, "Why not?"

"Because I'm not in a position to be able to evaluate my peers. I was busy with my own job and I didn't have a chance to observe them. I also don't have access to information that would tell me how well they're meeting their objectives or how satisfied their clients are. I had no facts on which to base an evaluation."

Megan yelled, "How dare you not follow my orders!" Then, through gritted teeth and in a staccato tempo, she continued, "Everyone else did it—everyone but you! What am I supposed to think of you now? How do you think I should evaluate *you* for not doing an assignment I gave you? And *you're* supposed to be a candidate for promotion?"

"Perhaps that's why I'm a candidate for promotion—I deal with facts; I don't speculate. And I do my job."

"Just leave! I'll deal with you later!"

I Promise

Relaxed and appearing genuinely concerned about the managers who report to her, Katrina addressed the group saying, "Welcome to our third annual department meeting. Based on your feedback from the last two meetings, I'm going to stick to the 6:00 PM end time, so you can count on having dinner with your families tonight—I promise. And just to be sure that I keep that promise, I've hired Rosa, a consultant, to facilitate this meeting for us. She's going to help us stay on track so that we cover all the points on our agenda and still end on time."

The meeting went smoothly until 5:45 p.m. when one of the managers asked, "Why haven't we discussed the results of our last audit? Isn't that important enough to share with the entire department? The results indicate that we have a huge problem, and since we have everyone together, this seems like a good time to address some of those issues."

Rosa responded, "That topic is not on your agenda. No time has been allocated for it. Do you think it can be addressed in the remaining 15 minutes?"

Katrina interjected, responding to Rosa's question, "This is an important topic, and I think we should at least begin to address it. We can still end on time and finish the discussion at another meeting."

Rosa said, "Okay then, here's what I propose you do in the remaining 15 minutes. First, someone can present the results to the group. Then I suggest that you cluster into groups of four. Each group can then generate three lists: a list of questions about the results; a list of possible causes for the results; and a list of recommended actions or solutions. I'll collect the lists at 6:00 and deliver a merged version to Katrina one week from today, along with a recommended agenda for the meeting at which you will continue the discussion. Please raise your hand if you agree to spend the remaining 15 minutes in this way."

All but two managers raised their hands. Rosa said, "Your decision is not unanimous. I think it would be beneficial to hear from the two people who do not agree. What are your concerns?"

One of the two managers said, "I don't think we can accomplish all of that in 15 minutes."

"What do you think can be accomplished?"

"I'm not even sure the results can be presented in the remaining time—we only have 10 minutes left now. I think the entire topic should be addressed in a separate meeting."

"Okay, before we get a response to your concern, let's hear the concerns of your colleague."

"I agree. This is a hot topic and I don't think it can be opened up and then shut down. Emotions are going to be running too high."

Katrina jumped up from her seat and dashed to the opposite end of the room from where Rosa was standing. Her face was red and her shoulders quivered as she hollered, "I've changed my mind! This meeting isn't going to end at 6:00! The audit is too important! We're going to stay until we've resolved the issues!"

Rosa responded, "You've given your word to these managers that you would end the meeting at 6 o'clock; they've made plans based on your promise. This doesn't seem to be an emergency. Are you going to break your promise for an issue that can be handled more effectively at another time?"

Members of the group whispered side comments that Rosa could hear, "Here we go again…" "This is so typical…" "We should have known not to trust her…" "Why should we expect it to be different just because a consultant is here…"

Katrina shot back at Rosa, "Thanks for your help today, I'll take it from here. You can go now."

I Need You to Stimulate Conflict

"I'm glad you could start today, Vaughn. It's a quiet time here and we can cover a lot of ground without being interrupted."

"Thanks, Jordan. I have a lot of questions."

"Well, I think I might answer many of them before you ask. I'm going to spend today going over the structure of the organization, the background of this department and how we've evolved to where we are today."

"Great. I'll take notes!"

"…That brings us to the current situation I'm experiencing with the managers who report to me. I was their peer and now I'm their boss. I'm making a lot of changes, but they won't speak up. I don't know what they're thinking but I know from when I was their peer that they don't approve of many of my ideas. That's part of the reason I created this internal consulting position and brought you in. I want you to challenge me in front of the group during staff meetings—ask a lot of questions. I want to show them that it's safe to speak up. I need you to stimulate conflict to help me create an environment of free exchange of ideas. I don't want them to think they can't challenge me because I'm the boss."

"No problem; I've always got plenty of questions!"

Vaughn began to meet with his peers to learn how he could support their operations. They each told him how the organization had evolved to where it is today and about the problems they were trying to overcome. Although he met with each manager individually, they all told the same story—a story that differed from the one Jordan told him and revealed an aspect of Jordan's personality that Vaughn had not yet seen. Each manager explained how they had all tried to help Jordan when he first became their boss. They said Jordan hadn't been with the organization very long before he was promoted and that they tried to teach him the business. They also said Jordan wouldn't listen to them. He had a preconceived idea about how he wanted to transform the department and he was overlooking the impact his changes would have on the organization's customers.

During one staff meeting at which Jordan presented the savings that would result from his newest idea, Vaughn asked, "How do you know that this is the right strategy? Have you done a study or a trial to see what happens?"

Jordan froze and glared at Vaughn. He ignored the question and continued. After a few minutes, Vaughn interjected again, "Jordan, I see where you're going with this, but I don't understand how people will get the information they need to do their jobs if you eliminate that position. Can you explain that part?"

Jordan responded, "Maybe we should meet in my office after this meeting. Everyone else knows what I'm talking about."

Jordan confronted Vaughn, "What was that all about?" he snapped. "Don't you understand that I need the support of these people? I don't need you raising doubts about what I'm doing. All you'll do is stir up conflict and make it harder for me to get them to go along with my plan!"

Vaughn responded, "Wait a minute; I'm just doing what you asked me to do."

"How do you figure that?"

"Don't you remember that when you hired me you told me you wanted me to stimulate conflict—to challenge you openly to help you create an environment of free exchange of ideas?"

Jordan ignored Vaughn's response and said, "I'm starting to have doubts about whether I hired the right person to do this job."

About These Examples

The "types" demonstrated in these stories are subject to interpretation. Several bad-boss descriptions may fit. It is not possible to characterize bad bosses accurately and with certainty without experiencing them over a period of weeks or months.

What Combination Types Want from You

Combination-Type Bosses want you to help them get away with doing whatever they want to do, whenever they want to do it. They want to look good to their management, and they want to take advantage of the organization for their personal benefit. They want you to pretend not to notice their inconsistencies. They expect you to adapt to their changing personality characteristics by changing your personality to match theirs; they want you to be playful with them when they're playful and obedient when they're dominant.

Combination-Type Bosses want you to make changes in your projects at their whim regardless of the consequences. They want you to forget what they said yesterday and never refer back to anything they've told you after they change their position or directions.

Combination-Type Bosses expect you to be passive and tolerate their quirks without question. They want you to acknowledge that they are of such a superior intellect that you cannot possibly comprehend their ways or keep up with them.

Reporting to a Combination Type Boss

Reporting to a Combination-Type Boss is like walking through a fun house at the circus; you don't know what to expect next. These bosses wear many masks and continually startle and surprise you in unpleasant ways. You can never be sure what type of personality characteristics your boss will exhibit when you arrive at work; whether you'll be flattered, ridiculed, or yelled at. Tension is constant. The entire tone of your department depends on your boss's mood and mode of operation on any particular day.

Combination-Type Bosses keep you in the dark as much as possible, not letting you know your organization's overall strategy so that you won't try to contribute any ideas—they run the show and you just take orders. Your Combination-Type Boss discounts your suggestions and may even laugh at them and call you naïve for offering them. He or she might say something like: "If you had any idea what was happening in this organization you wouldn't suggest something so irrelevant." When you ask what is happening, you get a response such as: "Let me worry about that; you just take care of the projects I give you."

Assignments are almost always confusing because of the contradictory and ever-changing instructions provided by your boss. Just when you think you understand what your boss expects, he or she tells you you've got it all wrong. When you express your frustration, your boss responds with statements similar to these:

- "You've got to learn to go with the flow."
- "You need to be more flexible."

- "You must understand that this is a changing business and you must change with it in order to keep up."

Your Combination-Type Boss never admits that he or she is asking you to make changes because of her or his misunderstanding, lack of knowledge, or interest in testing whimsical ideas. When you try to explain things your Combination-Type Boss does not know, he or she shuts you down and dismisses you.

If you are new to your organization and observing this erratic, bad-boss behavior for the first time, you may doubt yourself, disbelieving that it is actually happening. If you confront your boss, he or she will probably speak to you with a fake smile at first. Criticism will follow and its intensity will increase gradually. However, you will not be placed on a corrective course of action or threatened with termination. This is one of the ways by which Combination-Type Bosses give away their secret—they know their employees are right.

Combination Type Boss Survival Quiz

Examine your relationship with your Combination-Type Boss objectively in this "True-or-False" quiz:

Statement:	T	F
1. You are not bothered by your boss's different personalities on different days.		
2. You don't mind that your boss criticizes you for doing exactly what he or she instructed you to do.		
3. It does not concern you that your boss changes her or his instructions for a project several times while you are working on it.		
4. You are not confused by receiving praise from your boss for an idea on one day and ridicule for the same idea on another day.		
5. It is okay with you that your boss denies having said something to you after you quote it back to her or him.		
6. You do not mind having to determine your boss's mood before speaking to her or him.		
7. You are not bothered by your boss's contradictory explanations.		
8. You don't mind having to change your personality to match your boss's behavior on different days.		

If you responded "True" to most of these statements, there is a good chance you can survive reporting to a Combination-Type Boss without experiencing too much negative stress—as long as you can continue to adapt comfortably and avoid becoming the target of your boss's animosity or a scapegoat for her or his misdeeds. If your Combination-Type boss is just passing through your department on the way up the hierarchy, you have a good chance of surviving her or him for a year or a year-and-a-half until he or she is reassigned.

If you responded "False" to four or more of these statements, then it is very likely that you are already experiencing negative stress in your current position; you need to develop a strategy now.

Strategies for Surviving Your Combination Type Boss

You must take the time to determine which mode of behavior your boss is in before you interact with her or him on any given day. The more bad-boss types included in your boss's combination, the harder you must work at dealing effectively with your boss. The best strategy to use with your Combination-Type Boss will differ on different days, and sometimes at different times throughout the same day.

Be sure to focus on the things your boss *does and says*— things that you would be able to capture on video and audio recording devices if you were to use them—and *not* on the reasons *why* you think your boss may behave the way he or she does. Focusing on *why* your boss does what he or she does will not help you—you cannot change those reasons, and knowing them won't change your situation. Reasons are very complicated and individuals don't always know the real reasons behind their own behavior; even when they do, they're often unable to stop themselves without professional counseling.

Here are a few things you can do to maintain a fairly reasonable working relationship with your Combination-Type Boss:

- Identify the behavior pattern(s) most frequently exhibited by your boss. Use the strategies in each of the corresponding chapters in this book on days when your boss is in one of those modes.

- Start conversations casually with your boss, before you mention important issues, so you can get a sense of her or his "type" on any given day.

- Deal differently with your boss depending on her or his behavior each day; use the strategies listed in the chapter that corresponds to the type of behavior exhibited on that day.

- Always ask permission to think about assignments for a while and to renegotiate them later. Renegotiate questionable assignments on one of your boss's "better" days—he or she will be more likely to change the requirements then.

- Subtly praise your boss on good days to provide positive reinforcement for acceptable behavior, and withhold praise on bad days—do not question, challenge or criticize. Be pleasant on your boss's good days and neutral on bad days.

- Document all instructions your boss gives you and ask if you correctly understand them. If he or she has given you more than one set of instructions, provide a list of all of them each time you ask for clarification.

- Document your boss's responses to all of your questions for future reference to resolve misunderstandings.

- When your boss gives you explicit instructions to carry out, tell her or him in writing that you are proceeding according to your current understanding and list the details of your understanding in that memo.

- Network with peers who are not in collusion with your boss and whom you trust; develop informal support networks to help you acknowledge that your experience is real and that you do not deserve your boss's criticism.

Strategies That Won't Work

Do not confront Combination-Type Bosses with their contradictory or confusing behavior; they are likely to respond with anger. The more you try to prove your point, the worse you will be harassed. Your boss most likely knows exactly what he or she is doing and wants to get away with it. If your boss was unaware, then he or she would most likely not be able to maintain a consistent personality style with her or his managers.

Escalations will be of little benefit. Your boss's manager hired your boss. It is unlikely that your boss's manager will admit that he or she could have made such a mistake in hiring the kind of person you describe, and you will have little or no evidence to support your concern. You boss's manager knows your boss as a humble and loyal subordinate who reports the kind of results management wants. Your story will sound unbelievable, and you will most likely be referred back to your boss to work out your concerns with her or him directly.

Interview Strategies

What to listen for:

- *I need people who are flexible and can go with the flow.*
- *We don't always do things the company way in my department.*
- *Sometimes I'm still developing an idea while we're working on it.*
- *I like to try different approaches to things.*
- *Priorities change.*

All of these indicate that the interviewer could be a Combination-Type boss. If the manager says: "Priorities change," ask who controls the prioritization. If he or she responds: "I do," this could be a strong indication that the manager is a Combination-Type Boss. Changes in priorities from external sources such as customers and executives who determine the organization's strategy would not indicate a concern about this type.

Accepting the Consequences of Staying

Understand that if you decide to stay with a Combination-Type Boss, you will be subjected to her or his whims on a daily basis and must "walk on eggshells" to survive unscathed.

Before you decide whether to stay with a Combination-Type Boss, look at the severity of your situation mathematically. Let's say there are 240 work-days in a year, (based on a 5-day work week and allowing 4 weeks for holidays and vacation time). One day with a bad-boss per week (48 bad-boss days per year) equals 20% of your time at work. Two days with a bad-boss per month (24 bad-boss days a year) equals 10% of the time you spend at work. Add additional days for the lingering effects of your boss's behavior. Saying: "I am negatively affected by my boss 20% of the time" is much more powerful than saying: "I feel stressed out a lot of the time." Only you can determine what percentage is acceptable, and your tolerance level will probably depend on other factors in your life. The more stress you experience in other areas, the less you are likely to tolerate at work. There is no one-size-fits-all formula for determining when enough is enough.

If you choose to remain in an abusive or hostile situation with a bad boss, it may be helpful for you to become involved with other organizations where you can exercise your competence, be treated with dignity, and be recognized for your contributions. Becoming a volunteer, teaching something you know, and returning to school are excellent outlets because they require you to focus on other people and stop thinking so much about your bad situation—which can magnify if you constantly dwell on it. These activities can also help you preserve your self-esteem by overcoming or canceling-out any negative messages you get at work.

14: BASIC BAD-BOSS SURVIVAL STRATEGIES

Unless you are independently wealthy, supported financially by another person or a trust fund, working at your own business, receiving retirement or disability income, receiving welfare or similar social assistance, gambling successfully, or engaged in lucrative illegal activities, you need a job to get money. Getting a job means working at someone else's enterprise. If you work at someone else's enterprise, you will report to a boss. You can't always choose your boss and, even if you could, you can't always know in advance what kind of boss a person will be. The previous chapters explained how to get *along* with a bad boss. This chapter explains how to get *away* from a bad boss—without jeopardizing your income.

Both getting along and getting away from a bad boss are legitimate strategies for surviving your unpleasant circumstance and improving your situation. You do not have to stay in a bad situation, but you do have to plan and prepare to be able to make a break without sacrificing your lifestyle. This chapter tells you how to carry out three "get away" strategies:

1. Transfer Strategies

2. Resignation Strategies

3. Being Prepared to Resign: The Ultimate Bad-Boss Survival Strategy!

Most of us remain in dissatisfying situations as long as the positives (compensation, benefits and pleasant work associates) outweigh the negatives—the things we don't like but tolerate. It usually takes a dramatic shift, like a big increase in negatives or a big decrease in positives, to prompt us to take action to change our circumstances. The three strategies described in this chapter can help you make a move before the dramatic shift—before even worse things happen to you! Whether you support a family or just yourself,

227

these strategies can work for you. They do require an investment of your time and energy, but there is no quick and easy way to change the circumstances of your life.

1. TRANSFER STRATEGIES

Start with this True or False quiz:

The Transfer-Strategy Quiz	T	F
1. You like your organization—it's purpose, practices, offerings and opportunities.		
2. Your personal values are compatible with your organization's practices.		
3. There is at least one other department in your organization that interests you.		
4. You are certain that the boss who manages that department is not a "bad boss."		
5. You've uncovered facts that explain rumors you've heard about that department.		
6. Internal transfers are allowed and you know how the procedure works.		
7. You are qualified or can quickly become qualified to work in that department.		
8. You are certain that your current boss is the cause of your problems, *not* your organization's policies and practices.		

If you responded "False" to *any* of the statements in this quiz, then you either have more work to do before you decide to transfer or you already know that leaving the organization is a better option for you. If you think you're ready to resign, skip ahead to the "Resignation Strategies" section.

If you responded "True" to *all* of the statements in this quiz, then transferring to another job within your organization may be a good strategy for you. Now you need to prepare to approach your bad boss.

How to Initiate a Transfer Request with a Bad Boss

Asking for a transfer to another department can be a delicate matter. You need your boss's administrative support to make your transfer possible and you are creating additional work for your boss: preparing and signing papers, developing a final evaluation of your work, reassigning your current projects, advertising your position, interviewing candidates and training a replacement. For this reason, *never, ever,* under any circumstances, let a bad boss know that your reason for wanting to transfer is because of her or him! A boss who is angry with you or feels insulted by you won't be very willing to help you, and may even refuse to release you from your current responsibilities.

Always relate your reason for a transfer request to your organization's needs and goals and to your ability to satisfy those needs and goals. For example, you might say:

"I see that the accounting department is installing a new system. I believe my background in both accounting and information technology can help them get up to speed faster."

Be prepared to explain how the projects you are currently working on will be handled after you leave:

"My projects are all in the final stages and the Project Team Managers have all the information they need from our department. Jane and I back each other up and she can

229

respond to any questions that may come up about these projects."

Tailor your approach based on the length of time you've been in your current job. For example, if you are fairly new to your job, one way of relating your transfer request to you organization's needs and goals is to say:

"Now that I understand more about this job, I realize that I'm not the best person to do it. But I am better qualified for the vacant payroll position in the Human Resource department. I believe I can contribute more to the organization in that position, especially with what I have learned from you in the short time I have been here."

Be sensitive to the training investment your boss made in you. Explain how you believe that investment would not be wasted by focusing on the relevance of what you've learned to the new position (of course, there must be some element of truth to this reasoning.):

"I realize you've spent a lot of time training me to take phone orders. Because you've taught me so much about how the order entries relate to the fulfillment process, I believe I am ready to do that job."

If you've been in your job for quite a while, use a different approach, for example:

"I've been here now for two and a half years and I believe I've done the best job I can in this position. I would like the opportunity to learn more about the organization and apply my skills and the things I've learned from this job in the engineering department. I've found an available position that I'm qualified for, and I'd appreciate your support in helping me transfer."

Once again, your reasoning must have some element of truth to it and you must want to continue to work in your organization.

2. Resignation Strategies

If you've read the complete chapter or chapters that describe your bad boss, and if you've read the Transfer Strategies section of this chapter, then you know what you have to do. There's no reason to evaluate your decision—you've already determined the best strategy for your situation. The thing to do now is to be careful not to cause yourself any unnecessary problems.

Most job-search and career books cover the topics you need to know about conducting a job search, so that advice is not repeated here. Instead, these four rules are provided to help you get away from your bad boss with little or no negative impact:

Rule Number One:

Never, ever, under any circumstances tell a bad boss, or anyone else in your organization if you report to a bad boss, that you are planning to resign! If you've been a valuable contributor, your leaving is likely to hurt the organization, at least for a little while. Hurting the organization might make some people angry or even jealous—these are strong emotions. When people become emotional, they may do irrational things—things which may hurt your chances of making a smooth transition. So keep your plan to yourself.

Rule Number Two:

Don't feel guilty! Your bad boss is the cause of any hardship the organization experiences as a result of your resignation. Remember, it was your boss who wouldn't allow you to do your job in a way that supported the organization's goals. Your boss prohibited you from being loyal to your employer. You would have done the best job possible had you been permitted to do so. Hold your head high. You applied your skills and knowledge in exchange for compensation in the best way you could under undesirable circumstances. You don't owe anybody anything.

Rule Number Three:

Don't be hasty—unless your safety is threatened or you already have another source of comparable income.

Rule Number Four:

Make sure you are ready to resign. Read the next section and become familiar with The Ultimate Bad-Boss Survival Strategy. Determine which of the four aspects of that strategy apply to your situation and attend to them before you submit your resignation.

3. Being Prepared to Resign: The Ultimate Bad-Boss Survival Strategy!

During a workshop, a group of managers talked about their career goals. Ivan said, "My releasability date is a year away, so I'm not going anywhere for a while."

Emily, a new manager in the organization, asked, "What's a 'releasability date'"?

"When employees transfer into a new job in this company, they agree to work at that job for a period of time determined by their new manager. It's usually 18 to 24 months from the date they start, and sometimes longer. We call that our 'releasability date.'"

"Do you mean that if someone's in a job they don't like or don't do well, they have to stay in that job until the 18-to-24-months-or-more is up?"

"Yep, that's the way it works."

"And a manager would *want* them to stay?"

"Yeah. Managers don't want to spend all their time recruiting and training."

"That's crazy!"

"What do you mean?"

"I mean if I don't like a job, I'm leaving! Period! I'm outta here, even if it means quitting. I'll find a job or a boss I like somewhere else. And if any employee who reports to me doesn't like their job or doesn't do it well and wants to leave, I'm gonna help 'em go."

"You can't do that!"

"Who says?"

"It's against company policy!"

"Watch me."

Emily is prepared to execute The Ultimate Bad-Boss Survival Strategy.

Your Money **and** Your Life

The ultimate strategy for surviving Bad Bosses is to be prepared to leave any job at any time, and to be prepared to be unemployed at any time for a period of at least six months. That may sound like an enormous challenge, but it is possible and can be very worthwhile. Hostile and abusive work situations can result in economic losses as well as long-term health problems and shattered relationships.

There are four aspects to this strategy:

- Live Within Your Means.

- Self-Insure.

- Create an Independent Retirement Fund.

- Keep Your Skills Current.

A.   Live Within Your Means

Maintain a lifestyle that is achievable within your income level and do not acquire debt. If this doesn't seem possible, seek credit counseling from a reputable organization that can help you develop a workable plan.

Create and fund an account that will enable you to meet your living expenses for six to nine months in the event that you are unemployed for that long. Keep this fund separate from checking and savings accounts that you draw on routinely for living expenses and from long-term, limited access funds such as retirement plans. Seek advice from a reputable financial planner if necessary.

Consider working at a part-time job or starting a small business in addition to your regular job to help you build up the funds to get to a stage where you can live within your means. Starting a small business can be as easy as setting up an online auction account and selling products from your home.

B. Self-Insure

Many people feel they are "held hostage" by their employers in exchange for health and life insurance. To overcome this dependence, purchase health and life insurance individually, or join a professional association or similar organization through which you can purchase these benefits at group rates. This is a costly option, but it gives you the freedom to flee from hostility and oppression at any time with the security that major illnesses will be covered.

C. Create an Independent Retirement Fund

Open at least one Individual Retirement Account (IRA) and contribute to it regularly. Seek the advice of a reputable financial planner, preferably one who has no affiliation with a particular investment company and who is not compensated by the plans he or she recommends. While you cannot get the profit sharing benefits provided by an employer-sponsored 401K plan in an IRA, you can grow your investments with wise management. You can also transfer 401K or 403B balances from previous employers into an IRA.

D. Update Your Skills and Keep Current

One of your most valuable assets is your "employability"—the ability to get jobs quickly because you have skills that are sought by employers in the current labor market. Acquiring new skills is easier today than it has ever been. If you can read, you can learn. Books are an inexpensive way to learn. So are community college and many online courses. If the organization you work at offers training, participate in it. If tuition assistance is available, by all means, take advantage of it—knowledge and skills can never be taken away from you and they are the lifeblood of employability—invest in yourself.

If you are young and just starting out in the work force, you have the opportunity to develop quality-of-life habits that can help you survive unpleasant work situations throughout your life. If you are already established, you *can* change your lifestyle and improve your financial situation. Yes, you'll have to make sacrifices and work hard to change habits, but you will benefit in the long run. You must have a stronger desire for emotional security than material gain to make The Ultimate Bad-Boss Survival Strategy work for you.

APPENDIX: WHERE TO FIND HELP

Several resources are available to help you confront a bad boss and to provide emotional support for you. If you choose to confront your boss, realize that your situation may become worse before it improves—*if* it improves. If you choose to continue to report to a bad boss, emotional support can help relieve some of the pressure.

Inside Your Organization

Employee Assistance Program (EAP)

Many large organizations have internal counselors on staff or external counselors on contract who are available to offer guidance to employees about how to deal with difficult interpersonal issues. Check your organization's personnel manual or contact a Human Resource manager for a referral.

Pros	Cons
• Free. • Confidential—you are not required to tell a manager about the nature of your appointment. • Appointments may be scheduled during work hours. • Establishes a history of the problem.	• Counselors are usually prohibited from discussing your issue with anyone in your organization and may not be able to intervene on your behalf. • Sessions may be limited in time and quantity.

Human Resource Department (HR)

Managers in an organization's Human Resource department may facilitate escalations or contract an arbitrator to help resolve complex employee relations issues.

Pros	Cons
• Free. • Meet during work hours. • Learn about appropriate procedures to follow. • May arrange an interdepartmental transfer on your behalf. • Establishes a history of your complaint.	• Not confidential. • May require you to go through your management. • May be more inclined to protect the organization from charges they suspect you might file. • May not be qualified to address your issue.

Medical Department

Some large organizations have on-site or contracted medical facilities. Check with your Human Resource Department to determine if one is available.

Pros	Cons
• May diagnose and offer advice for treating stress-related illnesses. • Establishes a history of your condition. • May provide referrals.	• May not be qualified or allowed to counsel or advise employees. • Unlikely to confirm that the workplace is the cause of your condition.

Outside Your Organization

American Bar Association (Attorneys)

If your organization is unable or unwilling to help you, consider hiring an Employment Law attorney. Visit the Web site of the American Bar Association (ABA) at http://www.abanet.org/index.cfm. Click on the "Public Information" link to learn what legal assistance is available to you and to locate an attorney in your area, or call 1-800-285-2221 to obtain local information. Verify the standing of your attorney with the ABA state chapter.

Pros	Cons
• Can advise you about how to prepare documentation to support your claims. • Can determine whether you have a case for legal action against your boss or your organization. • May contact your management on your behalf. • May refer you to other helpful professionals.	• You must pay for services. • If your management finds out you've consulted an attorney, hostility may increase toward you or you may be terminated for contrived reasons. • You may be prohibited from resolving employee disputes through an attorney if you signed an employment agreement that requires arbitration.

Equal Employment Opportunity Commission (EEOC)

If you believe your boss or organization has discriminated against you, the Equal Employment Opportunity Commission may be able to intervene on your behalf. Visit the EEOC's Web site at http://www.eeoc.gov/ or call 1-800-669-4000, to determine if your case qualifies as "discrimination" according to law and to obtain local contact information.

Pros	Cons
• Free legal advice and assistance in employment-related matters. • Can help you determine whether your case qualifies as discrimination according to law. • Authorized to contact your employer on your behalf. • Establishes a history of your complaint.	• Discrimination is very difficult to prove. • Your organization's attorneys will be called in to work on your case and will work in the best interest of the organization. • EEOC agencies are frequently backlogged so it may be a while before they can get to your case.

To learn more about labor laws and governmental protection and agencies, visit the Web site of The U.S. Department of Labor at http://www.dol.gov/.

Family Members and Friends

Family and friends can be very supportive if you confide in them. Maintain a balance in your relationship; be there for them as much as they are for you and don't let your work issue overwhelm your relationships.

Pros	Cons
• Free. • Can help reduce tension and relieve stress. • Can help you refocus or direct your attention toward positive things.	• May become overwhelmed if you persist. • May find your story unbelievable. • May keep you from seeking professional help.

Psychological Services

Psychological services can help you deal with the impact that a bad boss may have on your health and social life. Visit the Web site of the American Psychological Association (APA) at http://www.apa.org/ and click on the "Consumer Help Center" link to learn more about psychological services and to locate a local professional.

Pros	Cons
• Can help you understand your role in your situation. • Can authorize a medical leave of absence. • Can refer you to a physician for medical treatment if necessary.	• You must pay unless your medical plan covers 100%. • Will not intervene on your behalf with members of your organization.

Religious Organizations

Many religious professionals are trained in counseling and can help their congregants deal with stressful situations. Contact a clergy member in your chosen religion.

Pros	Cons
• Free. • Can help reduce tension and relieve stress. • Can help you refocus or direct your attention toward positive things. • Can refer you to qualified professionals.	• Unable to diagnose medical conditions or recommend treatment. • Will not intervene on your behalf with members of your organization.

Other Books by Marilyn Haight

Kissing the Corporate Frog: An Enlightening Story about Leadership Traits 21st Century Employees Admire and Respect
ISBN 978-0-9800390-0-9.

The Instruction Writer's Guide: How to Explain How to Do Anything!
ISBN (prior to 2008) 978-0741426684
ISBN (after 2008) 978-0-9800390-2-9

E-Books

How to Spot a Bad Boss During an Interview
http://www.lulu.com/content/1385202

Who's Afraid of the Big, Bad Boss? is available by the chapter at Lulu.com. (Search by author's name or book title.)

Web Site and Blogs

BigBadBoss.com – Readers' stories with tailored advice
http://www.bigbadboss.com

Boss and Workplace Issues Blog
http://www.bigbadbossbook.blogspot.com

Bad Boss Poetry – http://www.poetryatwork.blogspot.com